Practical NLP 7: Business and Leadership

Book 7 in the *Practical NLP* series

ANDY SMITH

All rights reserved. This book was self-published by the author Andy Smith under Coaching Leaders. No part of this book may be reproduced in any form by any means without the express permission of the author. This includes reprints, excerpts, photocopying, recording, or any future means of reproducing text.

If you would like to do any of the above, please seek permission first by contacting us at coachingleaders.co.uk

Copyright © 2022 Andy Smith
All rights reserved.

CONTENTS

1.	Introduction	1
2.	Levels of Change	3
3.	Meta Programs	21
4.	Dealing With 'Difficult' People	46
5.	Feedback and Handling Criticism	60
6.	Changing States to Change Minds	65
7.	Running Better Meetings With NLP	70
8.	Negotiating: the 123-XL Model	81
9.	Selling (and Influencing) With NLP	91
10.	Leading With NLP	97
Index		101
Glossary of NLP Terms		104
About the Author		124
Books by Andy Smith		126

1. INTRODUCTION

This book follows on from the six previous volumes in the *Practical NLP* series, about Neuro-Linguistic Programming (NLP) principles, language, rapport and sensory systems, anchoring and submodalities, strategies, and reframing. We are getting even deeper into NLP now, so to get the best from this book you need to have at least a basic understanding of all of these NLP components, either from having read the previous books in the series (available at nlppod.com/books), or from reading and study with other NLP trainers.

To make it easier for you, I have added a glossary of NLP terms at the end of the book.

What Use Is NLP in Business?

Because business is mostly about dealing with people - listening to their needs, selling to them, motivating them, influencing them, and getting them to work together - everything you have learned so far in NLP is useful.

This book brings together some models and patterns that we haven't covered in previous books that will help you at work or in building your business. These include:

- the 'Levels of Change' (or 'Logical Levels') model for team building and successful organisational change

- some of the most useful 'meta programs' for understanding and influencing people in a business context

- suggestions for dealing with and even learning from difficult people

- why changing people's emotional states is an essential precursor to changing their minds

- how to run better meetings

- the 123-XL model for successful negotiations

- the CRAFT model for selling and influencing with NLP

- and NLP for leadership.

2. LEVELS OF CHANGE

You Can Analyse Change at Different Levels

How do you define yourself? Do you think of yourself mainly in terms of what you do? Or the skills you have? Or by what's important to you and what you believe? Or by who you are as a person? Or do you define yourself in terms of your purpose, or being part of something that's bigger and more important than you are?

To set the scene some more for this model that we're about to examine, let's use the perspective of problem-solving. Imagine someone who has real problems with his neighbours. It might get so bad that he decides to get out of that **Environment** altogether and move house.

If his new neighbours are also 'difficult', and he decides to move again, and once more he ends up next door to the 'neighbours from hell', you might begin to wonder if there is something he needs to change about his **Behaviour** in his dealings with other people, since he is the common factor in all of this.

If he doesn't know how else to behave, he may need to learn new skills or **Capabilities**: maybe some assertive communication, maybe a better way of dealing with conflicts, maybe even some rapport skills.

And if he believes that the way he has been behaving is the only right way to behave, he'll need to change his **Beliefs** before he can resolve the problem. If those beliefs are core to his **Identity**, he may have to rethink who he is in order to get a lasting resolution. And in order to get the impetus to do that - it's a big change, after all - he may have to start considering what is more important to him than he is to himself, or have some kind of road-to-Damascus **Spiritual** conversion.

This example illustrates the model devised by Robert Dilts that he called 'Logical Levels' or sometimes 'Neuro-Logical Levels', and we're calling "Levels of Change". Dilts suggests six levels or frames that you can use to analyse human experience, and particularly any problem or change.

LEVELS OF CHANGE

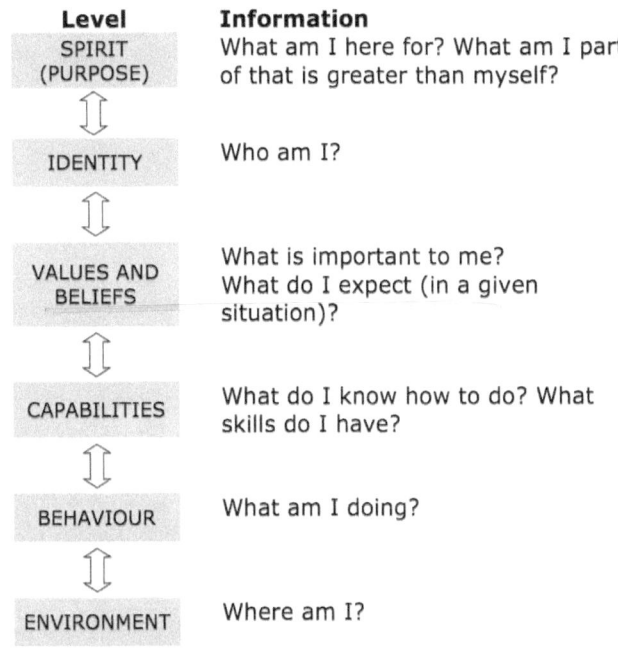

A good way to think about the levels of change model is to imagine a structure with a number of layers. The base layer is Environment - this is where you are, and what's around you - including other people. The fundamental questions here are "Where am I?" and "What is around me?"

The Environment level is the level of opportunities – but also of external threats. It includes where you work, where you live, and the people around you. If you're using this model to look at a business, the environment would include its market, its competitors, and the legal and regulatory framework it does business in.

The next level up is Behaviour. This is what you actually do - which of course takes place in, and acts upon, your Environment. The question here would be "What am I doing?"

Continuing upwards, the next level is Capability. If Behaviour is what you do, this is what you know *how* to do, what you are able to do - the skills that you have. So the Behaviour you put into action is chosen from within the range of possible behaviours covered by your skills. Just because you have the ability to do something, doesn't mean you will do it in any given situation, but as long as it's within your skill set, the behaviour is there for when you need it.

The next level up is Values and Beliefs: Values being what's important to you, and beliefs being what you believe about yourself, about other people, and about how the world works – so they govern how you make sense of what's happening and what's already happened, and also what you expect to happen next.

Your values are what motivate you - if a goal is important to you, you will put time and effort into making it happen - and they are also the criteria that you use to decide if something is right or wrong. The questions here would be "What is important to me?" (values) and "What do I expect? What do I believe?" (beliefs).

Beliefs include cause and effect linkages - you believe that a certain event is caused by something else, or that a particular action will cause certain consequences. We can also include your rules for yourself at this level - 'If this happens, I will do that'. Complex Equivalences - 'This means that', or 'This person or thing can be placed in that category' - are also beliefs.

Above Values and Beliefs, we have the level of Identity. This is the level of who you are, your sense of self. The question here, as you would expect, is "Who am I?"

Finally - and this is often left out of business NLP books for some reason, perhaps because the authors think it will scare the suits - we have the level of Purpose or Spirit. This is whatever you feel part of that is more important to you than you are to yourself; what you feel connected to, and what ultimately you would give up your life for. For some people this will be their religion, for other people it may be some political cause, or their country, or their family, or an idea - or it may be a combination of some of these elements, or there may be a gap there. If there is a gap there - if people haven't been focused on anything beyond themselves and their immediate problems - that's when you get people asking themselves questions like "Is that all there is?" or "What now?" when they've reached a goal they thought they wanted, or got far enough away from their problems that their 'away-from' motivation has run out.

Increasing Leverage

You will be familiar with the Einstein quotation that says something like "No problem can be solved with the same level of thinking that created them." I don't know whether he actually said that - he's the kind of iconic figure that people like to project their own views onto - but that quote could be tailor-made for this model.

If you remember our example of the guy with neighbour trouble, the symptoms of the trouble showed up at the Environment level. Trying to solve the problem at that same level, by moving to a different environment, didn't work, because the causes of the problem were located at least one level higher. Maybe it was how he was behaving, maybe he didn't have the capability to behave any differently, maybe he had the capability but didn't believe it was right to use it.

The way this model works is that the higher up the levels you go, the more leverage you have. A change at a lower level may affect the levels above it; a change at a higher level will definitely the levels below.

This is why a lot of corporate training courses don't stick - because they focus only on the Behaviour and Capability levels. Have you ever had a colleague who went on a course - maybe an assertiveness course or a management skills course - and their behaviour changed for a few days or weeks, but they soon slipped back into their old ways?

It's because they learned new skills (Capability level in this model) but their values, beliefs and sense of identity, the factors that govern whether they actually use those skills in a particular context, didn't change. Deep down, they wouldn't feel it was right to use their newly acquired skills, or it wasn't important enough to them, or using those skills just didn't feel authentic to them. Even though in theory they had a new range of skills and behaviour, in practice they reverted to the old ways.

So: if you're aiming to make change happen, make sure that the change is taking place at a sufficiently high level to make it stick.

Questions for Each Level

Each level in this model has particular questions associated with it, to direct your attention to a particular aspect of how a person, a team or an organisation is functioning - or to help you analyse a problem, or a success.

To get the most out of this section, ask yourself the following questions about your current job role, and notice what you learn from the answers.

The questions at the **Environment** level are, firstly, "Where" questions like "Where am I?" or "Where is this happening?" You can word the question differently, like "In what context does this problem occur?" but it's still really asking "Where?"

Another useful question at the Environment level is "What is around me?" or "What else is present?" You might find resources, opportunities or threats.

At the **Behaviour** level the question is "What am I doing?" What am I doing that contributes to or enables a problem, or a success? Of course, you could also ask what you are **not** doing that contributes to or enables the current situation. In relation to a goal, the question might be "What do I need to do to make this happen?"

As we move up to **Capabilities**, it prompts the question "What skills do I have that are relevant?" Also, "What skills do I need to get to where I want to be?" Or, for really minimalist questioning, "How?" as in "How can I do this? How can I make this happen?"

At the **Values and Beliefs** level, the basic questions are "What is important to me?" and more simply "Why?" or "Why do this?"

The question "Why?", though it's frowned upon in NLP when we're aiming to solve problems because the answers usually just restate the beliefs that helped the problem to happen in the first place, is useful here for precisely the same reason: the answers we get will illuminate our beliefs in relation to the issue.

At the **Identity** level the question is "Who?" as in "Who am I?" or "Who are we as a team?" (or an organisation). In relation to modelling successful performance you could ask "Who am I when I am doing this?" (or "Who are you" if you're modelling someone else's abilities). In relation to goals, or moving to a new level of success, you could ask "Who do I need to be to make this happen?"

At the level of **Purpose** or **Spirit**, the basic question is "For what purpose?" or "What's the highest purpose?"

You can ask this question in many different ways:

"What is more important to me than I am to myself?"

"In addition to that, what else?"

"What am I connected to beyond myself?"

"What greater reality am I part of?"

Coaching with Levels of Change

The intervention that follows is just one of many possible ways of using the model for coaching. This format is good for putting problems into perspective, and for uncovering purpose and motivation.

```
               SPIRITUAL/PURPOSE
                   IDENTITY              R
 P                                       E
 R                                       S
 O            VALUES AND BELIEFS         O
 B                                       U
 L                                       R
 E              CAPABILITIES             C
 M                                       E
 S                                       S
                 BEHAVIOUR
                ENVIRONMENT
```

(PROBLEMS / RESOURCES)

For any problem that the client has identified:

1. Lay out the levels of change on the floor – you could write the name of each level on a sheet of paper, or if you use the model a lot, make laminated

sheets that you can re-use. Ask the client to imagine that the problems at each level are on one side, and the resources at that level are on the other. Which side feels like the 'problem' side, and which feels like the 'resource' side? NB stand on the 'resource' side of the client, not the 'problem' side!

2. Ask the client to step on to the Environment level, reminding them what this level represents. Ask them to look at or step onto the 'problem' side and tell you what they notice at this level. Then ask them to look or step over to the 'resource' side – what is there at this level?

3. Step up a level and repeat the process for each level. When they reach the Spiritual or Purpose level (describe this level in accordance with the client's belief system), they will probably have reached an empowered state, transcending the original problem. Ask them to describe how they feel.

4. Ask them to keep that feeling with them as they turn and step down to the Identity level. How does what they found at the Spiritual level change what they previously found at the Identity level?

5. Keeping the feeling with them, get them repeat this process for each lower level. The original manifestation of the problem at Environment or Identity level should have gone.

6. Ask them to step off the Environment level. How will the future be different now?

N.B. if they encounter emotional problems at any level, as very occasionally happens, get them to step back down to a more comfortable level. Frame the emotions as valuable information and a basis for further exploration.

Levels of Change and Organisations

How does the Levels of Change model relate to organisations and businesses? For me, the relevance of the levels of change model to business really hit home when I joined a branding consultancy. I noticed that they often talked about 'brand values' and 'brand identity', and that reminded me of two of the levels of change. In fact, with a bit of thought I realised that the whole model is a useful way of looking at branding.

It was easier for me to see how the model relates to branding because we were focused mostly on service companies, where the brand and the organisational culture are the same thing, or at least should be. If the customer-facing brand and the internal culture of the company are different, the customer is going to notice the discrepancy every time they have contact with the company's employees.

You can understand the whole culture of an organisation, how it relates to its customers and competitors, and how that culture changes, in terms of levels of change. It doesn't matter whether the organisation is a small consultancy, a big multinational, a public sector organisation, or a charity.

Let's see how it works. The **Environment** level is the space in which the organisation operates. So it includes the customers (who may be segmented into several different markets), suppliers, joint venture partners, and competitors. It also includes external constraints like the legal framework and regulations that the organisation has to operate in.

Behaviour includes what the organisation does - not just making or selling things, but how it communicates with its customers and how it treats its own workforce.

Capabilities are the skills the organisation needs in order to perform the appropriate behaviours, and also to adapt itself in the face of change.

The organisation's **Values** are what's important to it, and also the criteria by which it decides whether it's doing a good job. In practical terms these translate into metrics and targets. The other side to values is that, in theory at least, they provide the motivation for what the company does. Where there's a gap between the organisation's values and the values of the individuals who work for it, there may be motivation problems.

Beliefs are what people in the organisation collectively believe about what they are doing. They are how people make some kind of sense of what they are doing and what's happening around them, and they're transmitted and maintained in at least two ways. One is by official pronouncements - by such means as the chairman's speech at a get-together, managerial pep talks delivered to a team, or those motivational posters you see which show some kind of noble animal or beautiful landscape together with a slogan that's meant to be inspiring.

The other way that beliefs are transmitted and maintained is unofficially, in the conversations that people have with each other (and with customers, suppliers and so on), and in the notices that people stick up on their own initiative like "You don't have to be mad to work here but it helps".

Beliefs are important: they form the map of the world that people in the company operates from, being woven and maintained moment to moment in day-to-day conversations. People will make the choices that make sense within their map, so what they believe has a direct effect on what they do. And you can probably guess which set of beliefs people will choose to adopt if there's a discrepancy between official and unofficial versions of reality.

The Identity level, of course, is about 'who we are' as an organisation. Every organisation has a sense of itself and its role. This is partly made up of ideas about what its intrinsic qualities are, and partly from how it sees itself compared to its competitors.

The **Spiritual** or **Purpose** level is about the and/or mission of the organisation - I'm saying and/or as there is no universally agreed definition of those two terms and they're often used interchangeably. Together, vision and/or mission are about the world that the organisation wants to see, and the manner in which it is going to get there.

This is important. In the 1994 book *Built to Last: Successful Habits of Visionary Companies*, Jim Collins and Jerry Porras identified a number of what they called 'visionary companies' that consistently outperformed the stock market - by a factor of 15 times from their starting date of 1926. The key difference between these visionary companies and their competitors was their focus on the company itself and what it stands for - its core ideology and purpose, its core values and the culture that puts the purpose and values into action.

In 'levels of change' terms, the focus of these visionary companies is on the upper levels of the model - on purpose, on identity, and on values and beliefs. By contrast, other companies which performed OK but not as well are focused more on the Environment level - on what they think their market wants and on what their competitors are doing or might do.

The organisations that really make a difference, that really create something new - as opposed to the me-toos and also-rans - focus on the difference they can make, and on being the best they can.

You may have noticed the way that original, one-of-a-kind movies that prove to be successful are often followed by a swarm of copycats that aren't as good. Like the pile of not-very-good British gangster movies came out after "Lock, Stock and Two Smoking Barrels" was a hit, or the long, dull, sword-and-sandal epics with huge computer-generated battle scenes that followed in the wake of "The Lord of the Rings". Or the way that Hollywood studios will always find it easier to make another sequel, each one worse than the last, rather than break new ground with an original movie idea.

That kind of output is what happens when organisations focus purely at the Environment level - what the market wants - rather than at the level of Purpose. But as that great innovator Steve Jobs of Apple says, "It's really hard to design products by focus groups. A lot of times, people don't know what they want until you show it to them."

When you focus at the higher levels of Purpose, Identity and Values, you can keep your motivation strong and adapt to changes in the marketplace and technological innovations while staying true to your essential nature.

Aligning the Levels

In order for an organisation (or a person) to be at its best, the levels need to be in aligned with each other. For example, if the organisation has 'Respect' and

'Integrity' as stated values (as Enron famously did in 1999) but treats its people badly or cheats its customers, what are people going to believe? What the company says, or what it does?

Identity, and Values and Beliefs, need to support the Purpose; the Behaviour also needs to support the Purpose, and the organisation may need to develop new Capabilities in order to be act in the way that's needed. When Identity, Values and Beliefs, Capabilities and Behaviour all line up to support the Purpose, the organisation has access to all of its resources and has the best possible shot at being able to cope with any challenges or competition in its Environment.

The best way to ensure that Values - and hence Identity - reflect the reality of the organisation's Behaviour is to involve people at all levels in crafting what they should be. That way, you keep it real and avoid the cynicism that results from 'espoused' values being too different from what happens in practice.

Levels of Change in Teams

You can use the Levels of Change model to tune-up the performance of a team by asking the team members to consider the team in the light of the different levels. Here are some example questions for each level.

Try this with your own team, or just have a go at answering the questions yourself now:

Purpose

What greater purpose (end goal) does the team contribute to?

What larger systems is it part of and how does it contribute to them?

What is its stated or unstated mission?

Identity

What is the identity of the team or organisation, and how strong is it?

How unified is the team's identity?

Values & Beliefs

What stated or unstated values and norms does the team subscribe to?

What stated or unstated assumptions does it operate from in practice?

What mechanisms allow these assumptions to be updated by experience?

Capabilities

What skills are needed to fulfil the mission and stated values of the team?

What skill needs does it have?

What skills do its members have that the team is not yet tapping into?

How does the team learn (from experience, and from best practice elsewhere)?

Behaviour

How closely do the actions of the team reflect its values and mission in practice:

- within the team

- outside the team, to customers, suppliers, other parts of the organisation?

What should it do more of?

What should it do less of?

Environment

How well does the physical environment of the team enable it to fulfil its mission?

What resource needs does it have?

What external constraints does it face?

3. META PROGRAMS

Meta Programs are one of the sets of filters we use to create our map of the world. They run 'in the background', so we are usually not consciously aware of them.

They drive:

- what we pay attention to
- what we respond to
- what motivates us
- how we interact with the people around us
- the kind of language that will influence us

As the name implies, Meta Programs are at a different logical level to our other mental 'programs' such as strategies. They influence the type of information fed into our strategies, the goals we set for ourselves, the way we make decisions, and the motivation behind our strategies.

When you understand meta programs, you will be able to see very quickly, from a minute or two's conversation with a person, what motivates that person and how to communicate with them in a way that makes it easy for them to understand - and act on - your suggestions.

The History of 'Meta Programs'

The term 'metaprogramming' first appeared in John C Lilly's book *Programming and Metaprogramming in the Human Computer* (1968). Lilly presented the human nervous system as a biological computer, running 'programs' either hard-wired or learned. 'Metaprogramming', as Lilly describes it, is changing the central control system so that we can learn more quickly and select more useful programs.

Richard Bandler introduced the idea of meta programs to NLP in the late 70s, as a way that people maintained coherency in their cognitive patterns.

Leslie Cameron-Bandler and others investigated further, using the Meta Model to identify a list of Meta Program patterns for use in therapy that eventually grew to around 60 in number. One of her students, Rodger Bailey, simplified the model into 14 patterns for use in a business context - the LAB Profile (Language and Behaviour patterns) as set out in Shelle Rose Charvet's excellent book *Words That Change Minds*.

Tad James and Wyatt Woodsmall's book *Time Line Therapy and The Basis of Personality* presents a very similar simplified set of patterns, and links them to Jungian personality characteristics as used in the Myers-Briggs Type Indicator.

What Meta Programs Are Not (although you'll sometimes find people using them as if they are):

- A way of putting people into boxes at the Identity level. Meta programs may be influenced by context and the person's emotional state.

- Either/or - instead, each meta program is like a spectrum and most people will be somewhere between the extreme ends.

- Absolute. Meta programs are context-dependent - for example, people tend to be more detail-focused about subjects that interest them.

Six Reasons You Need to Know About Meta Programs

1. **Achieving rapport**: meta programs are another thing you can match to help people feel at ease with you.

2. **Self-awareness**: if you are aware of your own meta program preferences, you will have a better idea about activities and career paths that allow you to play to your strengths.

3. **Recruitment**: every job has an ideal meta program profile. If you recruit people to match that profile, they will perform better in that role. You can even write job ads in a way that will attract the people you want, and put off the people that won't be suited to the job.

4. **Influencing**: you can use language that suits people's meta programs to influence them and communicate with them in the way that it is easiest for them to understand.

5. **Managing change**: describing changes in a way that is compatible with people's meta program profiles will make it easier for them to accept and feel enthusiastic about changes, and avoid triggering knee-jerk resistance.

6. **Sales**: you can help people to reach a buying decision by presenting them with information in the style and sequence that works for their meta program filters.

Detecting Meta Programs

Depending on the specific meta program, you can detect them from:

- The words that people use, the structure of their language patterns, and the way they talk.
- The way they behave.

- Their history, for example how frequently they have changed jobs.

Meta Programs in Business

Traditionally in NLP training, meta programs have been taught at Master Practitioner level. As far as I can tell, this is to do with the fact that they were discovered later than the 'classic' NLP components like submodalities and anchoring, rather than implying anything about their complexity or level of difficulty.

In fact, meta programs are easy to understand, recognise and use - and too useful to leave out of a business-oriented book on NLP. This book covers six of the most useful meta programs for business, with tips on how to identify them, job roles that different patterns may suit, and advice on how to influence and manage them.

You might also want to go back to the 'Convincer Channel' and 'Convincer Mode' in *Practical NLP 5: Strategies*. These patterns are also classed as meta programs but it was more useful to cover them under buying strategies, since that's what they are mainly used for.

A Note on Terminology

In books by British UK trainers you will often see 'meta programs' spelled as 'metaprogrammes', 'meta programmes', or 'meta-programmes'. Even allowing for the difference in US and UK spellings of 'program/programme', I prefer to stick with 'meta programs' because the term originates from an analogy with computer programs. When I worked in the IT industry in the UK, the US spelling was always used.

With regard to the titles of the individual meta programs, different books and trainers use different names. To make it easier to remember, I'm going to follow what many NLP Practitioners do informally and use the two ends of the spectrum of behaviour or attention that each meta program covers - so 'General/Specific' rather than 'Chunk Size Filter' or 'Scope' - although I will also mention the other names that you may see used for each meta program.

Towards/Away From (also known as 'Motivation Filter' or 'Motivation Direction')

Are you motivated towards goals, targets and what you desire, or away from problems and difficulties?

Extreme 'Towards' people will be gung-ho, and will overlook potential problems that can trip them up - think 'invasion of Iraq' or stock market booms.

People who are very 'Away-From' will be perceived as fault-finding and overly negative or cynical by their colleagues, and will lack direction unless given a problem to solve or a crisis to fix.

They also will run out of motivation the further away they get from what they wanted to avoid - so they might find it hard to lose that last eight pounds to get to their target weight, or they get close to their professed goals but let them slide before they finally attain them.

Like all meta programs, this one is context-dependent. You may find that someone is strongly 'Towards' or strongly 'Away-From' in almost all contexts that you ask about, or you may find that the same person varies in how 'Towards' or 'Away' they are depending on context.

Identifying the 'Towards/Away From' Pattern

Ask "What do you want in a job?" (or in a car, or relationship, or house). This will start to give you the person's values. For each value, you can ask "Why is that important to you?"

The answers will be either towards, away-from, or a mixture. Some values may be more towards or away-from than others.

Keep asking "Why is that important to you?" - at least three times. The initial answer is likely to be coloured by the prevailing culture - e.g. in the US you are likely to get a 'towards' answer than in the UK - so you need to go a bit deeper to find the person's real pattern.

Towards:
Language: talking about what they want, what they would like to see, what they can get, achieve, benefits.

Body language: nodding, gestures indicating the vision they are moving towards, 'inclusive' gestures.

Away-From:

Language: what to avoid, 'yes but', problems (including solving problems), pitfalls, avoiding, removing, "hang on a minute", comparative deletions, modal operators of impossibility, referring to target dates as 'deadlines'.

Body language: dismissive or 'warding off' gestures, shaking head.

Look out for 'concealed away-froms' in language patterns - the away-from is not explicitly mentioned but it's there in the person's internal representations:

- Comparative deletions e.g. "It's better to have money". Better than what?
- Modal operators of necessity e.g. "You've got to have money, haven't you?" What happens if you don't?

Job Role Examples

A "Towards" pattern is useful in: visionary leaders, entrepreneurs, creatives, ideas people. It's often found in change agents, coaches, and NLP Practitioners.

An "Away-from" pattern is useful in: health and safety officers, process control, proof-reading, maintenance engineers. Often found in medicine, pharmacy, solicitors, accountants, and bureaucracies of all kinds.

Influencing and Managing

Towards: this is what we can achieve, this is what it will get you, benefits, results, achievement, winning, advantages, what you can have, just think about it!

If you are an extreme 'Towards' person yourself, you may want to look at the massive benefits of doing an occasional 'minesweep' to make sure the route to your goals stays clear of potential problems.

Away-From: solve the problem, fix it, avoid, sort out, eliminate, this is what will happen unless we.., these will be the consequences if we don't do it.

If there are no immediate problems to motivate the Away-From person, ask them to look into the future to see the problems that will occur if they don't take action now.

Advertisements for cleaning products often use a lot of away-from imagery.

General/Specific (also known as 'Chunk Size Filter' or 'Scope')

What level or chunk size of information are you comfortable with - the big picture or the details?

This meta program is about which levels of the 'Hierarchy of Ideas' the person habitually focuses on.

A person at the 'General' end of the spectrum will think in terms of abstract concepts and generalisations rather than specific details.

When faced with too much detail they will feel overwhelmed or bored.

A person at the 'Specific' end of the spectrum will feel more comfortable with facts, details and step-by-step sequences. Abstractions, and the big picture on its own, will feel vague and nebulous to them without more details and specific examples.

Identifying the General/Specific Pattern

This pattern will come out in any general conversation. For an example, you could ask the person what they are currently working on, or how their day has been.

The 'Specific' person's answer will be in the form of a step-by-step narrative with lots of specific detail. They will use lots of qualifiers (adjectives and adverbs). If you interrupt them, they may start at the beginning again, or else re-start where they left off.

The 'General' person's answer will be shorter, in the form of a summary. It may not be in a temporal sequence, but will aim to give you what the speaker sees as the most important aspects first. This may seem like a random order to the listener.

Job Role Examples

Generally speaking, the higher level of abstraction a person can handle, the higher they can go in an organisational hierarchy (the upper ranks of the army are even called 'generals'). The ability to think strategically - in other words, to be able to work with high levels of abstraction - is usually essential for board-level roles. Having said that, people need to able to handle details to perform well at lower levels on their way up.

A detail focus is needed for: quality control, proofreading, health and safety, bookkeeping.

A big picture focus is needed for: leadership, creative roles.

Influencing and Managing

As with all the meta programs, match where the person is on the spectrum in order to communicate with them. If you need a 'General' person to be more specific, or vice versa, start from where they are and use pacing and leading to help them move up or down the levels of abstraction.

General: give the big picture, the overview, 'the real issue is...', 'in a nutshell'. Calibrate to notice if they are getting bored or overwhelmed with detail.

Specific: use examples and sequences (first..., second...), give detail, exactly, specifically, precisely.

Calibrate to notice if they are looking lost or if what you're saying is going over their head.

Proposals and reports often contain an executive summary (for 'General' readers) and appendices with lots of detail and facts (for 'Specific' readers).

Proactive/Reactive (also known as 'Action Filter' or 'Motivation Level')

Do you take the initiative and leap into action, or do you prefer to analyse and wait for others?

'Proactive' people are self-starters, and do not wait for others before they act. They are focused on achieving results and may upset others in their willingness to get there.

'Reactive' people won't act until they have analysed the situation, or until other people prod them into action. Other people may get frustrated with their apparent inactivity.

Identifying the Proactive/Reactive Pattern

This pattern will appear in language structure and body language.

Proactive

Language: Short, direct sentences, often with a 'command' tonality on statements or even questions. Active verbs. Active verbs and verb patterns indicating an 'at cause' mentality. Expects to be listened to. A need to act.

Body language: Generally fast. Fidgety, pencil-tapping, won't sit still for long periods (you will definitely notice this if you have a strongly 'Proactive' person in a meeting or training course).

Reactive

Language: Passive verbs, nominalisations, long sentences that tail off, verb patterns indicating an 'at effect' mentality (things happen to them, others 'make' them do things, lots of model operators of necessity). Conditional words like 'might', 'could', 'would'. Can have 'question' tonality on statements. A need to understand.

Body language: Able to sit still for long periods. May seek lots of eye contact - as if looking to others for approval or checking that they are being listened to.

Job Role Examples

A Proactive pattern is useful for: sales people (especially outgoing sales), business owners, leaders.

Proactive people need to be given things to do, otherwise they become bored. If you are recruiting for a role needing a Proactive pattern, you can screen out 'reactives' by requiring applicants to phone.

Don't hire highly Proactive people for jobs requiring diplomacy, or where consequences need thinking through.

A Reactive pattern is useful for: support desk, customer service, research and analysis, jobs which include long periods of waiting around.

Reactive people need time to get their heads round a decision, or to check how others feel about it. Don't hire them for roles requiring snap decisions.

Most job roles require a mixture of Proactive and Reactive.

Influencing and Managing

Proactive: use words about getting stuff done. 'Just' (as in 'just do it'), make it happen, let's get on with it, jump in, you'll smash it. Or Richard Branson's motto: "Screw it, let's do it." Pace their belief that they make things happen.

If you need to restrain them from jumping straight in, you can say "Just before we...." - the 'just' indicates that the delay will only be very short.

Give Proactive people ways to use their energy. If selling to them, give them a way of taking action or getting results straight away.

If you have a strongly proactive person on a course or in a meeting, make sure the activities or meeting segments are short. Even one Proactive person can disrupt things for others if they get bored and fidgety.

Reactive: use words about considering. As you consider, you could, we might, take as long as you need, circumstances are right, this is what you've been waiting for, everyone's doing it.

Use Cialdini's 'Social Proof' principle by giving examples of other people who have bought the product or are doing what you wanted them to do.

If you want them to act, use wording that implies that they have had a period in which to consider and analyse: now that you've had a chance to think about it, no need to wait any longer.

Internal/External (also known as 'Frame of Reference Filter' or 'Motivation Source')

This is about how much feedback you consider you need.

The Internally Referenced person has internal standards that they use to assess how well they are doing, regardless of what anyone else says.

The Externally Referenced person actively needs feedback from others to stay motivated and confident that they are doing a good job.

Identifying the Internal/External Pattern

This is a great question for a job interview: simply ask "How do you know when you are doing a good job?"

Internal: 'I just know', 'I feel it', 'My experience tells me', 'I decide'. They will refer to their own internal 'evidence'.

External: 'My manager/customers/colleagues tell me'.

For people in between the two extremes, you will get a mixture of the two answers, plus reference to objective external evidence e.g. that they hit their targets.

Job Role Examples

Internally Referenced people are good in back-office positions and those that require independent decision-making: leadership roles, technical specialists, the professions, creative artists.

Externally Referenced people are good in any front-line role: customer service, retail, travel, hospitality. Usually people become more internally-referenced as they spend time in a role and build up a 'database' of reference experiences to base their decisions on. Ideally, a person in a new role, or coming onto a training course (such as an NLP Practitioner course) will start out externally referenced and gradually become more internally referenced over time. This enables them to take on information in the early stages and become confident in applying what they have learned as they become more experienced.

Influencing and Managing

Internally Referenced: as you know, only you can decide, you may want to think about, this is just a suggestion, what do you want to have happen?

Externally Referenced: people are saying, research shows, they're not happy, this is what you could do, I've noticed that, the boss says.

Externally motivated people need frequent feedback. If they don't get any from their boss, they will become apprehensive as their annual appraisal gets nearer, because they literally will have no idea how they have been doing. If you are a strongly internally-referenced manager in charge of a strongly 'external' person, do whatever it takes to remember to give them more feedback than you would require yourself.

Externally-referenced people may take information or inquiries about the current state of some task as an instruction to do something about it, even if that's not what the inquirer intended.

Internally motivated people treat instructions from their manager as just more information; they will act as and when they see fit. Ideally, you will allow them to make their own decisions (or think they are making them, hence the use of influencing patterns such as 'only you can decide' - having set out the facts to point to a particular decision - and 'as you know' - before telling them something they don't know).

Find out what motivates the internally-referenced person and see that they get it. Feedback will not have much impact on them.

If you have a strongly internally-referenced person on a training course, you may have to arrange an experience that demonstrates to them that they don't already know everything there is to know about what they are supposed to be learning.

Sameness/Difference (also known as 'Relationship Filter' and 'Motivation Decision Factors')

This is about how people react to change and how often they need change. There are four main groupings along the spectrum from Sameness to Difference:

Sameness: these people like things to stay the same and dislike or actively resist disruption. According to Rodger Bailey's LAB Profile they will accept a major change every 10 years but only initiate change themselves (e.g. changing jobs) every 15 to 25 years.

Sameness with Exception: these people like things to stay the same, but with minor improvements or changes every so often. They like evolution rather than revolution. They need a major change every five to seven years.

Sameness with Exception and Difference: these people are comfortable with both large and small changes, as long as the major changes are no more frequent than three to four years.

Difference: these people like to switch jobs, roles or assignments very frequently. They flourish in rapidly changing environments and quickly become bored in the absence of change.

Identifying the Sameness/Difference Pattern

The classic question to identify Sameness/Difference for a given context (remember that as with any meta program, the degree of Sameness/Difference can change depending on the context), is: "What is the relationship between your work this year and last year?", or:

"What is the relationship between this job/house/whatever and the previous one?"

These are typical answers you might get from each of the four groupings in the pattern:

Sameness: will talk about similarities. "No change really - it's just the same as last year."

Sameness with Exception: will talk about similarities, but also mention some changes, often as comparisons. "I'm still doing pretty much the same thing, but I've been given a bit more responsibility and a new team member has joined." They will talk about how they got from there to here.

Sameness with Exception and Difference: may mention major changes and similarities, as well as using comparisons. "It's changed quite a lot since the merger; we're still expanding, and we're getting better at responding to customer queries."

Difference: may not understand the question - "What do you mean, relationship?" Will talk about what's different and new. "It's completely changed - we're in a whole new ballgame." They will talk about how things are now, rather than how things got to be how they are.

Job Role Examples

Sameness: roles that don't change are increasingly rare in the modern economy. In the past, this pattern would have suited administrative or clerical roles; nowadays, people with a strong 'sameness' pattern are likely to be viewed by managers as impediments to necessary change. Working with traditional crafts or the backwaters of retail may be the last refuges of the 'sameness' person.

Sameness with Exception: this is by far the largest category (65% according to Rodger Bailey) - will be comfortable in a role that changes gradually, where they can build on what has gone before.

Sameness with Exception and Difference: as for Sameness with Exception, but with the occasional major change as well, either in job role or employer/location.

Difference: the classic 'Difference' person is the management consultant, who takes on a new assignment every six months to a year - and gets frustrated when people in the client organisations don't embrace change enthusiastically!

Influencing and Managing

Sameness: as usual, continuity, reliable, similar, the same, tradition, heritage

Sameness with Exception: better, evolution, upgrade, development, improvement, the same except for...

Difference: revolutionary, new, paradigm shift, disruptor, unique, a whole new ballgame, totally different, new, game-changer

Sameness with Difference and Exception: use a combination of elements from the Sameness with Exception and the Difference patterns above.

To help Sameness and Sameness with Exception people to accept necessary changes, present the changes as small, evolutionary improvements that build on the best practice and successes of the past. The enthusiastic language of change advocates - "A revolution in how we do things! This is going to turn the whole business upside down!" - will not resonate with the majority of any workforce outside the high-tech sector.

Instead, you can find similarities and parallels between the new system and the old, and present it as basically the same with a few small enhancements, which will enable them to do what they've always done, but a bit easier and better.

Consider involving people in identifying which aspects of the current situation are working well and should be carried forward into the future to allay their fears of change (this is how the change method known as "Appreciative Inquiry" works).

When you are not able to give Difference-oriented people the substantive change they need to stay interested, you can at least change things around by rearranging the office and moving desks every so often.

Options/Procedures (also known as 'Reason Filter' or 'Motivation Reason')

This is about how you prefer to do your work. Do you look for alternatives and new ways of doing things, or do you prefer to follow the established procedures? Do you prefer to create new things, or maintain existing ones?

'Options' people, as the name implies, prefer to keep their options open, sometimes to the point of being reluctant to commit to a decision in case they lose out. 'Procedures' people like to have things settled and know where they stand. They like to complete and finish things.

Identifying the Options/Procedures Pattern

Generally, the modal operators a person uses will give you a lot of information about their pattern. Options people use modal operators of possibility ("can", "could") while Procedures people use a lot of modal operators of necessity ("must", "should", "ought", "needed to").

A good question to elicit someone's Options/Procedures pattern is "Why did you choose your current job?" (or in a house, or car, or whatever context you're eliciting the pattern for).

The Options person will use a lot of values in their explanation. They will talk about what they chose to do and why it was important to them.

The Procedures person will tell a story about how (rather than why) they came to be where they are. They talk about a sequence of events rather than choices, and don't mention their values.

Someone on the midpoint of the scale may tell you a story about how they got there, but also include references to the values or reasons why they made the choices they did.

Job Role Examples

Procedures people like to have instructions to follow and want to do things the right way. So they suit bureaucratic jobs, production environments, procedure-based areas of law like conveyancing, and professions like piloting where safety procedures are important.

Less obviously, sales people need a strong dose of 'Procedures' because success in sales is very largely about following tried and tested procedures, again and again. Franchisees need to be Procedures-oriented because franchises are all about following the instructions in the franchise manual.

Options people are reluctant to follow established procedures - deep down they believe there is always a better way of doing things. They get bored before they reach completion.

They are good in roles where creativity is needed - designers and design engineers, management consultants, and entrepreneurs. They would much rather start their own business than buy a franchise.

Some jobs, such as training and teaching, need a balance of Options and Procedures - options to be able to adapt in the moment and come up with creative ways of teaching things, procedures to be able to stick to a successful format or follow statutory procedures where necessary.

Managers also need an Options/Procedures balance to be able to manage staff with either profile.

Influencing and Managing
Options: improvements, possibilities, choice, reasons why, these are the options, a couple of alternatives

Find ways to allow Options people to exercise their creativity - get them to look at improvements to procedure or create something new.

Procedures: follow the procedure, first... then... and finally..., the right way, do it by the book, *n* steps to..., process, methodology

Procedures people do well with clear guidelines where they get to complete the process. Procedures are not just step-by-step sequences - they can also incorporate decision points and loop-backs (as in the TOTE model). The Procedures person can cope with this, as long as the directions for what to do in a particular situation are clear.

The impact of this pattern on selling, in brief: Options people are interested in alternatives, possibilities, and **why** they should buy something; Procedures people are concerned with **how** to use the product or service, and with going through the right steps to buy it.

There is much more about all of these meta programs and several others in Shelle Rose Charvet's very readable book *Words That Change Minds: Mastering the Language of Influence*.

4. DEALING WITH 'DIFFICULT' PEOPLE

Perceptual Positions

Now let's look at some ways of dealing with 'difficult' people. First, we're going to get some perspectives on a very useful NLP model known as 'Perceptual Positions'. The idea behind this is that if you look at something from a number of different viewpoints, you can gain extra information which gives you a basis for making wise choices.

The perceptual positions model is most useful in helping to improve relationships, especially in helping yourself and others to deal with those 'difficult' people (you know the ones I mean). Or those times when members of your family - even though you love them - can do or say something that really gets to you, or that you find hard to deal with.

Focusing on one of your 'difficult' people for a moment, and remembering that everyone has a different map of the world, and that no-one has a monopoly of the truth - who would that person say is the 'difficult' one in that relationship?

Here's the important thing about 'difficult' people: you can't change them. But that's OK, because it's not really them you have a problem with. Because we don't experience reality directly, and we filter our perceptions before we even become aware of them, you can never fully know another person - even the person you're closest to, let alone the ones we dislike and avoid as much as we can. It follows what you're having a problem with is not the difficult person him- or herself, it's your internal representation of them. And when you change your internal representation, you change your responses.

Looking at a relationship from the different perceptual positions is a way of gaining new information about it, making useful changes in your internal representation of the other person so you can deal with them more resourcefully, and gaining some additional self-awareness at the same time. Here's how it works.

You can look at any interaction with another person from three different viewpoints:

1. **Your own viewpoint** (sometimes known as 'first position'). This is a good position to be in for being in touch with your feelings and standing up for your own interests. Some people never grow beyond it.

2. **The other person's viewpoint** ('second position'). If you put yourself in the other person's shoes, you are more likely to understand how they see you and what their feelings and motivations are. This is extra information that you couldn't get if you stayed stuck in your own viewpoint. Do bear in mind though this 'mind reading' can only ever be speculation - you can't know for sure what

another person is thinking, although people often talk and behave as if they can.

3. **A detached observer's viewpoint** ('third position'). This is good for detaching yourself from the emotions of a situation and gaining a dispassionate overview. From this position you can observe the interactions between yourself and others as a whole system. You can see how you respond when they do something, and vice versa.

Disadvantages of Being Stuck in One Position

Sometimes people habitually experience things from one position only and miss out on the information available from the other positions.

If you always see things from your own point of view, you may appear selfish to others, and you won't understand how other people feel, or anticipate the consequences of your actions.

If someone sees things only from the other person's point of view, they become a 'doormat' because they put everyone else first and neglect their own feelings and interests. Other people will treat them accordingly.

Just take a moment to think: in the traditional Western nuclear family, who has - historically at least - most been in danger of falling into this trap? At mealtimes, who puts everyone else's food on the table and is still doing stuff in the kitchen when everyone else is sitting down to eat?

The 'third position' is about taking a detached overview. In the traditional 'command and control' workplace this is what managers are supposed to do: keep emotions out of decision-making and not let their feelings, or concern for others' feelings, intrude on the business of running things rationally. But if the manager always takes a detached overview, they will not be in touch with their own emotions and will have no understanding of others. They will appear 'cold' and lacking in humanity to other people. Research in the field of emotional intelligence (quoted in, for example, Daniel Goleman's book *Emotional Intelligence*) suggests that managers with greater self-awareness (which comes from the first position perspective) and greater empathy (which comes from second position) actually get better results - and this advantage increases the higher up the corporate ladder you go.

So wisdom comes from having the flexibility to move through the different positions, to see a situation from all sides before coming back to yourself to decide what you want.

Try Out Perceptual Positions for Yourself

On a decent live NLP training you will be able to explore perceptual positions in depth. For now, choose a recent conflict or disagreement, or a person you find difficult to deal with. Imagine the other person is somewhere in the room so you can see them. You are going to examine the situation from each of the three perceptual positions. If it's practical, you can mark out places in the room and physically move between them.

First, give yourself a couple of minutes to look at the situation from your own perspective. Notice what you feel about the other person, and what you believe to be true about them.

Now step out of that first position, noticing what you've learned, and do whatever it takes to leave that perspective and any negative feelings behind. Floating up above the situation, as far up as you need to go, often helps. So does distracting yourself - what is your phone number backwards? Only when you have completely detached from the emotions you normally feel in that situation is it time to do the next step.

Now, you know that other person. You know what they're like, how they stand, how they breathe, how they talk. Float down into that other person and 'become' them - in a method acting kind of way.

Now - looking back at the 'you' standing at the first position, what do you feel about them? What do you believe about the person in that first position?

Notice what you learn from this position and again, do whatever you need to do to detach yourself from that position and leave any feelings behind.

Finally, come down in a position which is an equal distance from the first and the second positions, so you can see both people in relation to each other. If you're not feeling fully detached from the first position yet - if you're still seeing it from your usual perspective - back off some way to get some distance, or stand on a chair to view it from higher up.

What do you notice from this perspective? Most people will find that they feel more resourceful about the situation, because they're viewing it from a detached perspective.

What do you notice about the interactions between the two people over there? Notice whatever you learn from this position. Also, what advice would you give to the person in first position? What could they do differently?

Now step out of that position, bringing any learnings with you. And come back to first position, and take as long as you need to integrate the learnings from the second and third positions into your experience.

What's different about that situation now? What's different about how you feel about it, and about the other person? What are you going to do differently next time you encounter that situation?

Finally, how are you going to use your knowledge of Perceptual Positions to make a difference to your relationships with others - or to help other people make a difference in their relationships?

Default Behaviours Under Pressure: The 'Satir Categories'

When you describe a person as difficult, what you're really saying is that you are finding it difficult to deal with that person at a particular time, in a particular context.

With somebody else, they may be fine. With you, in a different context, they may be fine. Even in the same context, there may be other factors present at that particular time which mean that you are finding them difficult at that moment. At other times in that context you may find them OK to deal with. So 'being difficult' is not an intrinsic quality of that person, and again if someone asked the other person "Who is the difficult one in this relationship?" they would probably say it was you.

It's also worth remembering that people are not their behaviour. At certain times, in certain contexts, they behave in a way that you find difficult - but it's just some behaviour that they're doing, it's not their identity.

Most of the time, when people are behaving in a way that you find hard to handle, it's because they're not in a resourceful state themselves.

The renowned family therapist Virginia Satir - who you will remember was one of the three therapists that Richard Bandler and John Grinder modelled at the start of NLP - noticed that people tend to fall into four recognisable ways of communicating and body posture when they are under stress - for example in arguments or disputes. Some people will find some or all of these four patterns of behaviour not easy to deal with.

One reason that it's useful for us to have a classification of these four behaviour patterns readily to hand is that being able to recognise a particular behaviour pattern as one of the Satir Categories gives us a bit of distance from the behaviour - "Oh, it's that" - so we don't experience it as quite as 'in your face', and we can stay in a more resourceful state so we can deal with it better. Also, being able to recognise someone's behaviour as conforming to one of the Satir Categories means we can prepare ways of dealing with it beforehand, so we're not always having to react automatically or trying to make up a response on the spot.

These are the original four patterns of behaviour under stress that Virginia Satir identified. Each one has its own distinctive body posture, behaviours, and type of language used:

1. The Placater
The automatic response of the Placater is to believe that everything is his or her fault. The Placater is always trying to please others, and always apologising. Their default way of dealing with confrontation is to cave in as soon as they're challenged.

Defining posture: symmetrical open physiology, looking up at you, arms outstretched, palms upward and moving up

Language: qualifiers - only, even, just, a little; could, would; "I don't know"

2. The Blamer

Loud, tyrannical, finger-pointing - it's always someone else's fault. The Blamer's voice is harsh and loud. This is just a guess, but they probably feel lonely inside. Their default strategy in confrontations is to attack.

Defining posture: In your face, leaning forward, pointing the finger at you

Language: universals - all, every, never; negative questions - "Why can't you ever listen?"; C➔E violations - "You're always making me angry"

3. The Computer

Dry, unemotional, super-reasonable, the Computer takes a detached view of everything. They stand rigidly, as if cut off from everything happening below the neck. The body is just a means to convey the brain from place to place. They often stand back with arms folded or one hand raised to the chin. The Computer can rationalise anything, retreating into abstractions to escape their feelings. Intellect is important to the Computer; feelings are not to be trusted. They will avoid confrontations, or any situation where emotions run high, if at all possible, and will try to hide behind logic, facts and the rule book.

Defining posture: rigid, leaning backwards

Language: Abstract words, passive voice, nominalisations; "There was an agreement" rather than "we agreed"

4. The Distracter

Always changing the subject, never answering a question directly, the Distracter feels ignored and will interrupt constantly to be noticed. They often have a repertoire of accents and funny voices - anything to avoid being serious or grown-up. Their way of dealing with confrontation is to use humour as a pattern interrupt.

Defining posture: asymmetrical, always moving, lopsided.

Identifying language: anything, as long as it's not relevant; "I don't know", "It's not my fault. The Distracter finds it easy to cycle through elements of the other four categories.

A fifth category was added later when Virginia observed that some people didn't go into an unresourceful state when under stress.

5. The Leveller

The Leveller presents as congruent, calm, solid, confident, authoritative. In confrontations they stand their ground and behave in an assertive but not aggressive way.

Defining posture: symmetrical, upright, centred, hands moving downward, palms down and spreading as if smoothing out or holding down troubled situations

Identifying language: "This is the way it is", "This is true".

Questions to Increase Your Self-Awareness

How you react when you encounter the different Satir Categories, and even how you feel when you think about them, can tell you a lot about yourself.

Try these questions:

Which of the Satir Categories do you tend to behave like when you're under stress?

Which of them would you feel really uncomfortable behaving like?

And which category do you want to use more of in future?

Learning From 'Difficult' People

The NLP presupposition you want to keep in mind here is "Behind every behaviour is a positive intention".

It's fairly easy to accept that every person, no matter what they do or how obnoxious their behaviour seems, is acting from a positive intention towards themselves. This belief helps to understand them and to let go of any anger or resentment we may feel towards them, as does imagining ourselves in their shoes.

But what would life be like if you believed, or at least acted 'as if', your aggressive customer, or belittling boss, or another driver who cuts you up, actually had a positive intention - not just for themselves, but towards you? Beliefs don't have to be true; they just have to be useful (having said that, of course they will stop being useful if they consistently contradict your experience, or are so incompatible with 'shared reality' that they interfere with your rapport with the people around you).

What would life be like if you believed that the positive intention of the inconsiderate motorist was to help you to learn to be a calmer driver? Would you be more likely to feel better and be more in control of the situation if you had that belief?

What if your whole life was a 'virtual reality interactive training package'? So that everything that happened to you was designed to teach you something - if you don't learn what you need to learn from a challenge the first time, life will go on presenting you with that challenge in different forms until you do learn what needs to be learned and can move on to the next learning. Would that be a useful belief to help you to learn from experience?

Use this process next time you encounter a person you find 'difficult'.

First, ask yourself: What is the positive intention behind their behaviour? Put yourself in their shoes and see things from their point of view (NB don't do this with seriously disturbed people). See yourself briefly through their eyes. What do you learn from this different viewpoint?

Then, ask yourself: If there was a positive intention towards you behind that person's behaviour, what would that positive intention be? What positive lessons do you need to learn from your interaction with that person?

We often project qualities or characteristics we dislike onto another person. As you are responding to your internal representation of the person, rather than the person themselves, guess where the annoying characteristic really is? Within you! So it can be useful, if sometimes uncomfortable, to add a third step to the process:

Finally, ask yourself, "How am I like that person? When do I behave like that?"

5. FEEDBACK AND HANDLING CRITICISM

Giving Effective Feedback

What's your purpose in giving feedback? If it's to unload your own feelings, or to make yourself feel more important by attempting to make the other person feel small, or to get revenge on the other person for some previous comment that you took as a slight or a put down, be aware that this is going to damage your relationship with that person - and also, if that kind of behaviour goes against your values, it will probably damage your relationship with yourself.

The only legitimate reason for giving feedback is to change the other person's behaviour - and you need to be aware that whatever your intentions, if the person on the receiving end perceives that you're doing it to unload or to put them down, that message will not be received as sent. Either the person will get defensive and dig their heels in, or they'll feel crushed and unresourceful. Either way, you're not going to see the behaviour change you want, because lasting behaviour change requires learning, and people can't learn when they are angry or upset.

So, assuming that your motive genuinely is behaviour change, here are some ways to give feedback effectively. The principle here is that a person's behaviour is not the person - if someone is behaving in a way you don't like, you want to accept the person and change the behaviour.

Rather than using the term 'constructive criticism' - which is still criticism, and will bring out an unhelpful emotional reaction unless the person is completely emotionally detached from their behaviour - I'm going to say 'stating what you would like someone to do differently'. It will be easier for them to take on board if it is accompanied by praise. This applies whether you are coaching other people or looking back at what you yourself did in a particular situation.

1. Use the 'Agreement Frame'

Instead of the often-used format which follows positives with a 'but' and some criticism (effectively wiping out the positives before the 'but'), use the 'Agreement Frame' format:

"Overall, the presentation got the result it needed to, and I think it would have gone even better if you had taken a moment to centre yourself before you started."

2. The 'Sandwich'

This format wraps the criticism up in two compliments, making it even easier to swallow.

1. Start with what you liked about what the other person did.
2. Then tell them what you would like them to change about what they did (if anything).
3. Tell them more about what you liked.

If you use this model 'mechanically', people could end up expecting a criticism as soon as they hear any praise. To prevent this, just give praise or positive feedback on its own whenever it is due.

Focus your feedback on what you would like to change about the person's behaviour, rather than criticising the actual person. In this way the person (or you, if you are reviewing your own performance) stays motivated and in a good learning state.

Feedback aimed at identity rather than behaviour is, as you would expect, more likely to be taken personally. If a person is upset because they feel criticised at the Identity level, they are less likely to be in a good state to learn what they need to learn - or may even dig their heels in and refuse to take any of it on board.

Strategies For Learning From Criticism

So what if you're on the receiving end of criticism, or feedback where the giver isn't skilled in giving it? Here are some strategies you can use. You'll notice how they use submodalities or framing to make it easier to take on board whatever there is to be learned, while remaining in a good state.

1. The easy way:

When someone criticises you, do you accept it and take it to heart, or do you keep it at arm's length to examine it first? When someone praises you, do you accept it and take it to heart, or do you keep it at arm's length to examine it first?

Hands up if your default response is to accept the criticism automatically, but stop praise at a distance and examine it for accuracy. What would happen if you tried doing it the opposite way?

Accept praise and take it in uncritically. "What if they don't mean it?" you may ask. Do it anyway. Do it more! It will drive them nuts.

When you get criticism, stop it at arm's length in your perceptual space and examine it before accepting it. How justified is the criticism? What really happened? How qualified is this person to offer feedback?

2. If you're being heavily criticised, you need to maintain your state.

Centre yourself and imagine an 'energy bubble' around you that deflects all criticism, stress and negative emotions. Take all criticisms as applying to the behaviour level only, no matter how they are phrased.

Later, when it's safe to do so, examine the criticisms using one or both of the next two options.

3. Decide what 'Level of Change' you are going to take the criticism at - regardless of the level that the critic has aimed it at.

4. Take a detached view:

Dissociate from your 'other self' receiving the criticism (float up above).

Keep the 'other self' in a resourceful state. Run movies of what the critic is saying, and your experience of what happened, and compare them. Learn what you need to learn and discard the rest.

6. CHANGING STATES TO CHANGE MINDS

Most of what we do in business is about influencing people and getting them to make the right decisions. Whether it's selling, so that they decide to choose your product or service; or passing interviews, so that they decide it's you they're going to hire; negotiating a better price from your suppliers; getting a productive outcome from a meeting; or leading people so that they perform better than they would by themselves.

To achieve any of this, it's important to realise something that many of those 'Influence with NLP' and 'Get Anyone to Do Anything You Want!' courses out there don't tell you, which is the most important thing you need to know about changing people's minds.

It's this: the emotional state that your audience are in will have more bearing on the outcome of your meeting or presentation than any fancy language patterns or persuasion tricks you may have up your sleeve.

As the marketing guru Seth Godin says in a typically insightful piece on his blog, it's almost impossible to change people's minds when they've already made their minds up and are determined not to change (http://bit.ly/sethchange).

Seth describes how he was at the airport on standby, desperately needing to make his meeting in Buffalo. When someone ahead of him in the standby queue gets a seat, he offers her $100 to give him her seat and take the next flight, only 90 minutes later. She turns him down without a thought, as do the next two people. He doesn't manage to get on the flight.

Why weren't the other passengers open to this generous offer of getting paid $65 an hour to read a novel? Because they'd had their hopes set on getting a seat on the earlier flight for an hour, and when their name was called to say they'd got it, they weren't going to give that up. They'd already made their minds up.

As Seth says, the same thing happens in business.

There's no point at all in holding a meeting aimed at bringing about change if the people in the meeting have insulated themselves against changing their minds.

And as he points out, the conference room acts as an anchor for that 'no-change' insulated state. As soon as people walk into the room, they are reminded that this is somewhere you stand your ground, you don't back down, and you don't want to look indecisive.

He suggests two ways you can combat this effect, and we can add a couple more:

1. Pick an audience who are in the mood to 'flip' as he calls it - in other words, change their minds. For example, people who have just moved to a new town, started a new job, or bought a new car. This is excellent advice. Even more in a mood to 'flip' are people who are looking to change their job or buy a new car.

   When I was looking to get out of a day job that I hated, back in 1992 (it was in IT since you ask), I responded to an ad in a newspaper that turned out to be for a hypnotherapy course (although it was headed 'Become a Stress Auditor'). It was a very expensive course (later on I found the content was of a pretty low standard too, but I had no standards to judge by back then) - but because I was definitely in the mood for a total career change, they didn't have much trouble signing me up for it.

2. "Start a cascade of small flips". Robert Cialdini's excellent book *Influence: The Psychology of Persuasion* describes a psychology experiment by Freedman and Fraser in the mid-60's found that householders were almost six times as likely to agree to have a large, ugly "Drive Safely" billboard on their front lawn if they had earlier been asked to display a

three-inch-square "Be a safe driver" sign in their front window.

This was an example of Cialdini's 'Consistency Principle'. Displaying the small sign changed the self-image of the householders; once they'd put the small sign up, they started thinking of themselves as public-spirited citizens and were much more likely to agree to the larger request in order to maintain consistency with their new self-images.

3. As we said, office meeting rooms tend to be act as anchors for a closed, inflexible mindset. So, how do we collapse that anchor, or at least give it a chance to wear off? One way might be to remind people of when they were in a more open state, when they had just made a change or were about to make a change - when they first joined the company, the last time they were looking for a new car, when they moved to a new town or a new country.

   People use examples, stories and metaphors all the time to get their point across, so why not design some of your stories to take your audience back to a time when they were ready to make a change? And if the story has a happy ending, so much the better.

4. If you're speaking to an audience on a training course, you could also use a quick rhetorical question, brain-teaser or physical activity to act as

a pattern interrupt. For example, you could get them to try crossing their arms the opposite way to how they normally do it. This is why trainers have 'icebreaker' exercises at the beginning of their sessions.

However you do it, make sure people are in a receptive state before you start trying to persuade them.

7. RUNNING BETTER MEETINGS WITH NLP

Let's look at how we can use NLP to run better meetings, and to have the meeting turn out the way you want it to more often.

Do you sometimes find yourself in meetings that drag on, don't achieve as much as they should, in which people seem to be bored and disengaged?

When I was an employee, I took part in a lot of unproductive meetings. Sad to say, I probably chaired a few as well. Later, I discovered NLP and realised that there are certain things you can do to make your meetings run better, get things done, and make people feel that they are actually worthwhile attending.

In some businesses and professions, people spend more time in meetings than they do actually working. A doctor mate of mine used to do a stress management presentation for overworked general practitioners. One of the slides was captioned "Meetings: the practical alternative to work". So if you want your meetings to work better, keep reading.

But first, and to help you make these tips your own, let me ask you a question: from what you already know of NLP, what could help you to run better meetings? I can certainly think of a few ideas from NLP which could help and I'm sure you can too.

Mainly, as with anything you set out to do, follow the 'Three Pillars of NLP' - know your desired outcome, maintain your sensory acuity so you notice what's going on, and have the flexibility to change what you're doing if you need to. Now let's get down to specifics.

If we think of a meeting as having three stages: preparation, opening the meeting, and during the meeting (including closing), here are three frameworks, one for each stage, which will help you run emotionally intelligent meetings that don't eat into productive time. Things are always easier to remember with acronyms, so get ready to remember... MODEM, RASTA and, er, DRUBS.

Preparation: "MODEM"

1. **M**ust we meet? Is the meeting necessary?

Meetings, preparing for meetings, and travelling to and from meetings, take up a lot of time that often could be more productively spent elsewhere.

Considering meetings in the light of the "Managers vs Makers" distinction made by Paul Graham at paulgraham.com:

- Meetings fit well with someone on "Manager's schedule" where the day is divided into one-hour intervals.
- "Makers" (programmers, technicians etc) need longer chunks of time to be productive. For them, a 10:30 AM meeting means switching work modes, and breaks up the morning into chunks that are too small to accomplish anything non-trivial in.

Information updates can be handled by email or phone. Anything with an emotional impact needs a face-to-face meeting.

2. **O**utcome: establish where you want to get to by the end of the meeting.

"This is what I want to happen by the end of this meeting."

Use the 'Evidence Frame' and ask: What will you see/hear/feel that tells you that you have achieved your desired outcome? What will be measurably different?

If you know what you want to get from the meeting, it makes it much more likely that you will be happy with the end result. There's also another effect of being outcome-focused in meetings which may surprise you - for some people at least it dispels their nerves.

I had a coaching client who, despite being a successful marketing manager for a multinational corporation, felt nervous in meetings and had trouble speaking up. I asked her what her desired outcome for her main weekly meeting was and she said "Not getting found out."

Now, we could have spent some time going into her feelings about authority figures and identifying her limiting beliefs, reframing them, and clearing them, but for some reason we didn't go down that route. Instead, I asked her if it made a difference to her what the meeting decided (if it turned out that it didn't make any difference, I was going to ask her if she actually needed to attend the meeting).

I got a very congruent "Yes" response - it mattered a lot to her what the meeting decided. So I asked her to do some work before the next meeting on getting very clear on what she wanted to happen and the outcome she wanted to see.

The next week, she reported back that not only had she not felt nervous, but she had spoken up several times and the meeting had agreed on the outcome she wanted. As soon as she focused on her desired outcome, her attention shifted from internal (on her own feelings) to external (onto the other people in the meeting, looking for evidence that the meeting was going the way she wanted). When you are focused on what you want to happen, you're not concerned with the ups and downs of your own feelings, and you are literally unselfconscious - which puts you into a more resourceful state.

3. Decide what you will do for each foreseeable contingency

Explore what could happen and establish "if-then" options for what you will do if it does. "If the IT suppliers object that they don't have capacity to implement the proposal, I will identify some existing tasks that can move down the priority ladder."

Even better, if you know that someone is likely to raise a particular objection, you can preframe it out when you introduce your agenda topic in the meeting to head off the objection before it happens: "I recognise that the new project will place additional demands on IT, so if necessary we can identify some existing tasks that can take lower priority..."

4. Establish who needs to be there, and agree the agenda

Discover the desired outcomes of the people who need to be at the meeting and get their agreement on the agenda. If you've missed anything that's important, this is their opportunity to get their concerns raised in the meeting.

5. **M**eeting place

Make the environment conducive to the outcome you want. Choose a place where you won't be interrupted and people won't be called away.

The closer the seating arrangements are to being in a circle, so everyone can see each other's eyes, the more participation you will encourage.

To really make sure that people concentrate and don't waste time, have the meeting standing up.

Opening the Meeting: "RASTA"

1. **R**apport

As people come in, greet them and establish rapport with them. This will make them feel more part of the meeting and engaged in a collaborative venture rather than a contest to get their objectives accepted. It will also encourage them to open up and be less guarded when it is their turn to speak.

2. **A**wareness (Sensory Acuity)

Calibrate the physiology of people in the meeting. Ideally you are looking for alert, responsive people. If someone appears to be in the grip of a negative emotion, this could disrupt their concentration or even the whole meeting if you don't deal with it.

If you do notice that someone appears to be stressed or anxious, you can ask them about it. Frame your question in a way that does not imply weakness or deficiency on their part, as that could provoke a defensive reaction. Ask "Is there a situation you need to deal with before we start the meeting?" rather than "What are you worried about?" or "Is your attention 100% on the meeting?" They might, for example, have left their car in a restricted parking area and be worried that it will get towed. They will be much more productive if they are allowed to deal with whatever is bothering them before the meeting starts.

Throughout the meeting, use your peripheral vision to regularly check for external signs (changes in facial expression, breathing rate and so on) of changes in the emotional states of participants. This will give you some feedback about how the meeting is going.

3. State and agree the outcome and evidence procedure

"This is where we want to get to by the end of the meeting, and we will know when we've got there because..." Check for understanding and agreement around the table.

4. Time frame

Make sure everyone knows that the time that the meeting has to end. Ensure that everyone has time to say what they need to.

5. Achievements: start with successes

With team meetings, use the "Appreciative Frame". A good way to get people into a better (and therefore more capable and creative) state is to ask "What successes and achievements have we had since we last met?"

This should be in the spirit of an invitation to contribute, rather than picking on individuals like this: "You! What have you achieved?"

For more detail on the Appreciative Frame and other frames in NLP, see *Practical NLP 6: Parts, Frames, And Reframing*.

During the Meeting and Closing: "DRUBS"

1. Detail - get the right level

For productive meetings, make sure the discussion is operating at the right 'chunk size'. Discuss ideas, objectives and responsibilities rather than every little detail of how someone is going to achieve them. If details need to be discussed, this can be done outside the meeting.

Remember, the more you drill down into detail, the longer your meeting will take, the less interesting it gets for people not directly involved in that topic, and the more opportunities you have for people to disagree.

2. **R**elevancy Challenge: how to keep the meeting on track

Make the agenda and the desired outcome explicit. Write the agenda out and put it up on the wall where people can see it.

If any participant goes off on a tangent, you can respectfully challenge: "Excuse me, how is this relevant to the agenda/outcome we agreed on?" and point to the agenda.

Pretty soon, just a nod or gesture to the agenda should be enough to bring people back on track without you having to say anything.

3. **U**nproductive participants: how to deal with them

We can identify two types of unproductive participants: someone who has 'switched off' and is not paying attention to the meeting, and someone who is actively objecting and nit-picking.

If the person appears to have 'switched off', you need to establish what is going on for them.

Are they worried about something outside the meeting? Consider allowing them some time out of the meeting to deal with it (see the 'Awareness' step in RASTA above).

Are they thinking they shouldn't be in the meeting? If this were the case, ideally you would find this out beforehand. Consider letting them leave if they don't need to be there for the rest of the meeting, and their responsibilities and actions have already been established.

If this happens regularly, with more than one person, take it as evidence that your meetings are too long or that you are inviting the wrong people.

If the person is constantly raising objections (a mismatcher or polarity responder), they are not necessarily doing this to be deliberately obstructive. They may feel compelled to find flaws in arguments or to present the opposing point of view to restore a sense of balance.

A graceful way of dealing with mismatchers is to give them the job of "devil's advocate". Ask them to make notes of any flaws or objections they notice, and allocate some time at the end of the meeting for them to report back on what they found.

4. 'Backtrack Frame' to handle disagreement

If there is major disagreement or objection at any stage, try this: interrupt and summarise what has been agreed up to now, starting from the beginning of the meeting and continuing up to the last point of agreement. Match the vocal tonality of the objector to pace and then lead them towards a calmer state.

In effect, this 'rewinds' the meeting to the point before the disagreement broke out, and is an opportunity to start over on the controversial area.

5. **S**ummarise

At the end of the meeting, summarise what has been agreed, who is going to carry out each action and the completion date. You could also do a mini- summary at the end of each stage.

Confirm the date for the next meeting and thank the participants.

8. NEGOTIATING: THE 123-XL MODEL

For negotiating, I think it's again useful for your understanding to ask what you have learned from NLP already that might be useful in getting better results from negotiation? If you come up with some things that I don't mention in this chapter, so much the better.

Here's a model for negotiation that I've called the '123-XL' model. See how many of the NLP elements you recognise in it. Before we start, I will say that the most important thing you can do to improve your negotiating skills is to practice, so that you build up positive reference experiences of successful negotiating and being a good negotiator.

We're going to look at negotiating as a three-stage process: preparation, the negotiation itself, and the subsequent review of what happened to see what you can learn from it. The 123-XL model is spread across these three stages.

Preparation

1st Position: What do you want?

Before you go into a negotiation, it's vital to know your ideal desired outcome.

This will give you a starting point for deciding your opening offer, which will be some way beyond what you would happily settle for.

Then establish what is your 'Best Alternative To A Negotiated Agreement' (BATNA) - what you could get without negotiating? This will give you the lower limit or walk away point of your negotiating position.

If the BATNA is better in every way than what you could get from negotiating, you don't need to enter into negotiation.

To develop unity among your negotiating team, chunk up to what is important to you about your desired outcome. Are these values shared by all the significant players on your side? If not, chunk up further until you reach what unites you.

You already know what you think your desired outcome is. What other options than this initial outcome could satisfy the values you have established? Develop as many satisfactory options as possible, to avoid being stuck in a single negotiating position.

2nd Position: What does the other side want?

Learn as much as you can about the other side. If you don't have reliable information, you'll have to use your imagination. Put yourself in their shoes and imagine how things look from their point of view.

- What is their ideal desired outcome?
- What is their BATNA?
- What are the values behind their negotiating position?
- Are these values shared by all their negotiating team?
- Are there divisions you could use?
- What other negotiating positions could satisfy their values (bear in mind that the other side may not have thought of all of these yet)?

Anticipate possible objections to your proposals, and think of ways to preframe them out.

All the way through the negotiation, you should be checking your initial estimates of the other side's position against how they actually behave, and filling in any gaps with this new knowledge.

3rd Position: Look at the positions of the two sides from an objective viewpoint, without attachment to the outcome.

From this perspective, how important is it to maintain the relationship? What would be the future consequences of maintaining, strengthening, or dissolving the relationship? What would be the potential gains and losses?

If the relationship is worth maintaining, what would be the best outcome for the relationship? Aim for a "win/win/win" solution where you, the other side, and the relationship between you all benefit.

What areas of agreement exist? What areas are still to be resolved? Plan how to discuss them.

People tend to go into negotiations regarding the other parties as adversaries, so employ a different frame: what would the situation look like if the two sides were collaborating in finding a resolution?

The Negotiation Itself

EXchange

Everything that happens in the actual negotiation is potentially useful information that you can use to update your knowledge of the other side's position.

a. At the opening of the meeting, establish rapport.

b. Make sure you are negotiating with the right person - one who can make a decision. Ask something along the lines of: "If we discuss this today and we decide that we can reach some sort of agreement, will you need to consult someone else to get their approval, or are you able to make that decision yourself today?"

If the approval of another person is needed, you need that person to be present at the negotiation.

c. Explore the outcomes and values behind their negotiating position by using an 'as if' frame: "If we were to arrive at some sort of agreement, what would that look like?"

d. Early on, establish the areas of agreement, and summarise any progress made up to this point. Emphasise shared interests and shared values.

e. State the areas to be resolved.

f. As areas of disagreement or objections come up during the negotiation process, probe for the outcomes and values behind them.

g. Develop win/win options that dovetail the desired outcomes and values of both parties.

h. Get agreement on the best option.

i. Close: summarise the agreement and agree an action plan.

Common Tactical Errors When Negotiating - and What to Do Instead

1. **Opening with your minimum acceptable position, or close to it.**

   This is a classic error of inexperienced 'amiables' or people-pleasers when they try to negotiate. Deep down they are worried about being rejected and that the other person won't like them – which means that someone who doesn't care about being liked can walk all over them. Remember, once you've gone down, you can't go back up again. Instead, open with your 'ideal' position.

2. **Taking rejection personally.**

   The other side are rejecting or objecting to your proposal, or some part of it, not you as a human being. If you notice yourself having a pattern of being concerned about this, being clear about your desired outcome will help.

3. **Not maintaining your own state.**

   Excessive adrenalin produces the fight/flight/freeze response, which is not conducive to win/win outcomes. Fear and anger states reduce your ability to reframe, put things in perspective, develop new ideas, and absorb new information. Maintain a positive state by centring, peripheral vision, dissociating when necessary, and being kind to your body by getting enough sleep, exercising when you get the chance, and avoiding excessive coffee, sugar and alcohol.

4. **Losing rapport.**

    Examples would be using judgemental language about your opponents or their proposals - "This is a laughable offer" - or making accusations - "You're being really obstructive."

    Instead, use "I" language that takes responsibility for what you're saying, and talk about consequences and how you feel about them:

    "A figure as low as that will not provide an incentive to invest, and I feel concerned about the long-term viability."

    Notice that statements about how you feel can't be contradicted.

    Another way to lose rapport is to use personalising language - so talk about "that offer" rather than "your offer" if you need to raise objections. Also, explicitly label your suggestions and questions to help the other side see them as just those, rather than as sneaky tactics: "Let me ask a question at this point"; "I'd like to offer a suggestion."

5. **Framing the negotiation as a fight rather than a collaborative search for a solution.**

    If you aim to crush your 'opponent', even if you succeed, the best you can expect is remorse, resentment, and revenge. The classic example Gregory Bateson gives in *Steps to an Ecology of Mind* is the Treaty of Versailles after the First World War, where the victorious Allied powers humiliated the defeated Germany with a treaty so harsh that it created the conditions for the rise of Nazism and another world war within twenty years.

Instead, you can frame the negotiation as a shared search for solutions. You can ask for help in developing options for mutual gain, present a number of options for the other party to select from, or agree standards for selecting an option.

If the other side present unacceptable options or appear to be 'fighting dirty', it can help you to separate the positive intentions behind their behaviour from the behaviour itself. Just like you, they are doing the best they can. What can you do to make it possible for them to act in a more acceptable way?

6. **Negotiating with your team in view of the other team.**

    If you make divisions obvious, it's easy for the other team to exploit them. If you need more time, ask for a recess.

Other Useful Tactics

Anchor any states that occur for later use. For example, if the other side seem more receptive for some reason, use a word or even a gesture that they will unconsciously associate with that state. If the association is strong enough, you will be able to lead them back into that state whenever you want by using that word or gesture. The interesting thing here is that you don't need to know the reasons their receptive state came about in the first place in order to anchor and use it.

Preframe your proposals with reason and explanation, rather than making the proposal and giving the reasons for it afterwards.

Give at most two strong reasons for your proposal, rather than a whole list of reasons. The more reasons you give, the more opportunity the other side has to select the weakest reason and object to it.

One way of handling an objection is to ignore it and act as if it never happened. If the other side doesn't raise it again, it was a tactic rather than a genuine objection.

Use the 'Agreement Frame': "I agree (or 'respect' or 'appreciate') and..." rather than "but...". You can find more about the Agreement Frame in *Practical NLP 6: Parts, Frames, And Reframing*.

Test understanding and more importantly re-establish rapport by paraphrasing: "So you're concerned about our long-term commitment to the project?"

Use the 'Backtrack Frame' to summarise what's been agreed so far, stopping before any current sticking point.

Remind the other side of shared interests, values and outcomes (chunking up for agreement).

Review

Learn from what happened:

- What went well? What will you definitely do again next time? What will you do differently next time?

- With anything that went wrong, "What do we need to learn from this?"

- Where you have encountered unexpected objections, develop ways of preframing them out next time.

Note: the 123-XL model was developed by me, Andy Smith.

Recommended Books on Negotiation:

Getting to Yes by Roger Fisher and William Ury (not an NLP book)

Influencing with Integrity by Genie Z Laborde – has a good chapter on negotiations.

9. SELLING (AND INFLUENCING) WITH NLP

There are two aspects to success in sales - one is the 'numbers game', which is about getting people into your sales funnel and actually contacting the customer. Given a certain ratio of sales to number of contacts, the more customers you contact, the more sales you make.

If you already have a proven sales model in place, work with it. Follow the steps (in a Procedural fashion) and you will get results. The key to success here is taking action, and there are various NLP tools you can use to manage your state and help you stay motivated:

- **Anchoring** to get yourself into a motivated state
- **Swish Pattern** to defuse any negative triggers that hinder you from getting started
- **Reframing** to keep your motivation going (for example, remembering that it takes a certain

number of "nos" to get to a "yes", so each "no" is good because gets you closer to the next "yes")

- **Reframing**, along with **Submodalities Belief Change**, can also help you to let go of limiting beliefs that get in the way of selling, and of taking rejection personally

- **Submodality shifts** to transform, defuse or eliminate altogether any critical internal dialogue

- **Parts Integration** to increase your congruence about selling

- **The Appreciative Frame** to help you remember, learn from, and build on your successes

- **Modelling** to help you learn from sales superstars

- The **New Behaviour Generator** to help you develop and take on new, more effective behaviours.

You may have your own favourite tools from NLP for state management.

The other key factor in sales success is establishing a relationship with your customer, understanding their needs, and convincing them to buy from you at the right time, rather than from someone else at some undefined point in the future.

The CRAFT model that follows is designed to give you a structure that helps you do this. If you have your own proven sales model already in place, you can take the

NLP tactics included in the CRAFT model and apply them to your own process to turbocharge your results.

One more thing about the CRAFT model; as well as sales, it also applies to any form of influencing or persuasion, because when you're influencing someone, you're really selling them the change in their behaviour or mindset that you want to happen. So we could equally well call it the 'CRAFT model of influence'.

The CRAFT Model of Influence

1. Credibility

Establish your credibility by making sure you are congruent, managing your state, projecting authority, and using command tonality when appropriate (and making sure you don't use a questioning tonality when making statements).

Anticipate and preframe out potential objections (give credible examples that counter objections before the customer even thinks of them). Each time you hear a new objection, develop a preframe for it to use next time.

Get to know your customer's industry sector (or, in business to consumer sales, understand their circumstances) so that you understand the terminology they use.

2. **R**apport

Establish rapport by being responsive and friendly, understanding your customer, matching their general speed and energy levels, using open body language and a positive voice tone, and above all - pay attention to the customer.

Notice what you can about the customer's values, and their preferred representational system.

3. **A**way-Froms

Establish or discover the problems that the customer faces. In conventional (non-NLP) terms, this is where you get a better understanding of the customer's needs.

By the end of this stage (and also drawing on information gathered in the Rapport stage), you will want to have found out about:

- Something they bought that they are happy with, and how they bought it (this should give you their Convincer Channel, Convincer Strategy and their Reassurance Strategy). Anchor this feeling of reassurance, so you can use it later.

- Something they bought that turned out to be a bad purchase (also anchor this so you can use it later).

- What their internal representation of success is, and what they want to avoid.

- Their values.

If your offering genuinely doesn't offer a solution to their problems, tell them honestly (this will enhance your credibility and strengthen your relationship for the future - the customer will see you as an adviser who has saved them from making a costly mistake) and move on to the next customer.

4. Future Implications

Explore and emphasise what will happen if they *don't* make a change. You are aiming to ramp up the customer's away-from motivation here. Go as far into the future as you need to in order to get the customer to realise the seriousness of their problems and the need to do something about them now.

5. Towards Your Proposed Solution

Present your proposed solution. Use 'because' to give reasons to hit both towards and away-from values. Only present the benefits and features that are relevant to the customer's perceived needs.

Subtly use the 'Reassurance' anchor if they are considering buying your offering, and the 'Bad Purchase' anchor if they are considering the competition's offer. The key word here is 'subtly'; in fact, it may be best to let your unconscious mind handle this chore, which will happen anyway if you really believe your product is better than the competition's.

Important - bear in mind that being "caught" using any kind of NLP tactics that the customer sees as manipulative is an instant rapport and credibility killer. Even if buyers are not trained in NLP themselves (and an increasing number are), they will unconsciously pick up if you are not genuinely trying to help them solve their problems.

10. LEADING WITH NLP

How can NLP help you become a better leader? It's tempting to say "all of the above" - you can use everything that you've learned through this book, and the whole *Practical NLP* series, to lead better in one context or another. It will be worth your while to take a moment to consider: what are the most important things that you've learned from NLP that will help you be a better leader?

I want to highlight a couple of things that we've touched on before, and as you consider them again, I wonder what new and additional learnings will come to you?

Firstly, the importance of congruence - integrity - in a leader. When you heal any internal conflicts or dilemmas you might have had, you become more effective as a leader. With parts integration, and getting all the levels of change in alignment, you now have ways of doing that.

Gandhi said "you must be the change you wish to see in the world" - in other words, the most effective form of leading is leading by example. What others see of your leadership is the result not just of your conscious intentions but also your unconscious actions, so the more aligned you are within, the more effective you will be at getting the results you want in the world around you.

Secondly, remember your effect on the emotional climate of your team or your business. As you know, the leader of a team has more effect than anyone else on its emotional climate, because in times of uncertainty, people look to the leader for clues as to how they should behave.

You don't just lead by example when you're physically present - even the stories that people hear about you can affect their behaviour, for good or ill.

Let's take blaming others as an example of the kind of behaviour that can be influenced. A study by the University of Southern California's Nathanael Fast and Stanford's Larissa Tiedens asked people to read a report about the 2005 ballot defeat of Governor Schwarzenegger's efforts to reshape the state government of California. In one version of the report, the governor blamed special interests for the defeat, while in another version he took full responsibility.

The researchers then asked the participants to write a short essay to explain a time in their lives when they had failed. The participants who had read the article about Schwarzenegger blaming special interests blamed others twice as much for their own personal failures. Repeating the experiment with blaming and non-blaming versions of other articles about failures gave a similar result. (Blame contagion: The automatic transmission of self-serving attributions in *Journal of Experimental Social Psychology* 46 2010 97–106)

Let's be clear about this - Arnie wasn't their immediate boss, just a leader that the study participants read about. How much more influence is what you say and do going to have on the people who actually report to you?

So remember what you can do to improve the 'emotional climate' of your team:

1. Lead by example. Keep yourself in a resourceful state whenever you need to, using anchoring, submodalities, and all the other state management tools you've learned.

A "resonant" leader creates a positive mood throughout the organisation, their example encouraging everyone to contribute their best efforts. A "dissonant" leader who engenders a climate of anxiety and doubt - through undermining people, outbursts of anger, or a consistently gloomy attitude - acts as a brake on the performance of the whole organisation.

2. It's OK to show emotion. The more expressive the leader (in facial expression, voice tone, and gesture), the more influence he or she will have on the overall emotional climate. Inexpressive, stone-faced, monotone bosses create an 'emotional power vacuum' that a more junior but more expressive team member can step into and become the 'emotional team leader'.

3. Even if you are not the nominal leader, you can still have a positive influence on the emotional climate. If your boss has left an 'emotional power vacuum', it is even more important that you maintain yourself in a positive state. This will 'resonate' with your colleagues and influence them to feel and perform better.

4. Finally, the most effective leaders are those who can communicate a vision that inspires people and resonates with their values. In the next book in this series, we'll find out how to elicit values and set goals that are truly compelling.

INDEX

A

Action Filter, 32
Anchors, 66, 68, 89, 91, 94-95, 99

B

Bailey, Rodger, 22, 38, 40
Bandler, Richard, 22, 53
Bateson, Gregory, 88
Behaviour level, *see* Levels of Change

C

Cameron-Bandler, Leslie, 22
Charvet, Shelle Rose, 22, 45
Chunk Size Filter, 29
Cialdini, Robert, 34, 67-68
Convincer Channel, 25, 94
Convincer Mode, 25
Convincer Strategy, 94
Credibility, 93, 95-96
Criticism, 60-64

D

Difficult people, 3, 46-59
    Learning from, 57-59
Dilts, Robert, 4

F

Feedback, 35-37, 60-64
    Learning from critical, 62-64
    'Sandwich', 62
Frame of Reference Filter, 35
Frames, 4, 13, 75-77, 84, 88
    Agreement, 61, 89
    Appreciative, 77, 92
    'As If', 85
    Backtrack, 79-80

Evidence, 72

G

Godin, Seth, 66
Grinder, John, 53

I

Identity level, *see* Levels of Change
Influencing, 21, 24-25, 29, 31, 34, 36-37, 40, 44-45, 65-69, 91-96, 99-100

J

James, Tad, 23
Jobs, Steve, 17

L

Leadership, 28, 31, 33, 36, 65, 97-100
    'Dissonant' vs 'Resonant', 99
    Visionary leaders, 28, 100
Levels of Change, 3-20
    Aligning, 17-18
    And organisations, 13-17
    And teams, 18-20
    Behaviour level, 4, 6, 8-10, 14, 18, 20, 61-63
    Capabilities level, 4, 10, 14, 18-19
    Coaching with, 11-13
    Environment level, 3, 5-6, 8-10, 12-14, 16-18, 20
    Identity level, 4, 7, 9-10, 12-13, 15-19, 23, 62
    Questions for, 9-11
    Spirit or Purpose level, 4, 7, 11-12, 16-19
    Values and Beliefs level, 4, 6-7, 9-10, 13-20
Lilly, John C, 22
'Logical Levels', 4

M

Meetings, 32, 34, 65-66, 68, 70-80
Meta programs, 21-45
    Detecting, 24
    General/Specific, 29-31
    Internal/External, 35-37
    Options/Procedures, 42-45
    Proactive/Reactive, 32-35
    Sameness/Difference, 38-42
    Towards/Away From, 26-29
Motivation, 6-7, 11, 14-15, 17, 21-22, 48, 62, 91
    Away-From, 7, 26-29, 90
    Motivation Decision Factors, 38
    Motivation Direction, 26

Motivation Filter, 26
Motivation Level, 32
Motivation Reason, 42
Motivation Source, 35
Towards, 26-29, 95
Myers-Briggs Type Indicator, 23

N

Negotiating, 65, 81-90
'Neuro-Logical Levels', 4

P

Perceptual Positions, 46-52
Peripheral vision, 76, 86
Preframing, 74, 83, 89-90, 93

R

Rapport, 4, 23, 58, 75, 84, 87, 90, 94, 96
Reassurance, 94-95
Recruitment, 24, 33
Reframing, 73, 86, 91-92
Relationships, 27, 46-47, 52, 53, 60, 84, 92, 95
Relationship Filter, 38

S

Sales, 24, 33-34, 43, 45, 65, 91-96
Satir, Virginia, 53

Satir Categories, 53-57
   Blamer, 55
   Computer, 55-56
   Distracter, 56
   Leveller, 56-57
   Placater, 54-55
Schwarzenegger, Arnold, 98-99
Self-awareness, 23, 47, 50, 57
Spirit or Purpose level, *see* Levels of Change
Strategic thinking, 30
Strategies, 21, 25
   Convincer strategy, 94
   For learning from criticism, 62-64
   Reassurance strategy, 94
Submodalities, 63, 92, 99

T

TOTE Model, 45
Treaty of Versailles, 88

V

Values, 27, 43, 60, 82-83, 85, 90, 94-95, 100
   Values and Beliefs level, *see* Levels of Change
Vision, 16, 28, 100

W

Woodsmall, Wyatt, 23

GLOSSARY OF NLP TERMS

Analogue

1. Describes a representation that corresponds to what it is representing. So a picture of a dog looks like a dog. The sound of a bark sounds like a dog – and the louder and deeper the bark is, the larger you might reasonably expect the dog to be. The opposite of digital; a digital representation of a dog, for example the word 'dog', looks nothing like a dog. All sensory representations are analogue.

2. Of submodalities, describes a submodality for which degrees of intensity are possible (rather than the 'one or the other' of a digital submodality). For example, a picture can be 'light' or 'dark' or any point in between.

Anchor

The neurological link between an internal state or response and an external stimulus (e.g. a smell that evokes a memory). Anchors can be set up accidentally in the course of a person's life or be installed (or removed, or chained to a sequence of other anchors) deliberately.

Associated

To view a memory or imagined event from within, through your own eyes. This typically gives more access to your feelings in the event than if you are dissociated.

Auditory

Refers to the sense of hearing. If someone is in 'auditory mode' they are paying more attention to what they hear than to other senses and using the sense of sound as their primary method of processing information.

Auditory Digital

Processing in internal dialogue.

Calibration

Noticing the non-verbal signals that a person gives off, particularly with the aim of detecting changes from the initial 'baseline' as a sign of changes in the person's state.

Cause and Effect

A *Meta Model* pattern stating or implying that one event caused another, whether or not this is actually the case, as in "You make me angry." Often used as a way of avoiding responsibility for one's actions.

Chaining Anchors
> The process of setting up a sequence of anchors such that setting off one anchor automatically leads to the next one in the sequence being set off. Useful for pulling yourself out of a 'stuck state' like apathy or boredom.

Chunk
> A quantity of information that a person processes as a single item in their working memory.

Chunking
> How the person divides the information available into chunks for processing it.

Chunking Down
> Moving from the big picture and abstractions to details and more concrete observations.

Chunking Up
> Moving from details and the concrete to abstractions and the big picture.

Collapsing Anchors
> The process of getting rid of an existing negative *anchor* by setting off a more powerful positive anchor at the same time. The more powerful 'positive' anchor 'blows out' the negative one, as they can't coexist.

Comparative Deletion
> A *Meta Model* pattern where something is compared to something else, but the thing being compared to

is not stated. E.g. "I'm much better" invites the question "Better than what?"

Complex Equivalence

A *Meta Model* pattern stating or implying that one thing (or action or concept) is the same as or is a sign of some other thing, action or concept, where the link may only exist in the mind of that person. E.g. "You don't bring me presents, you don't love me."

Congruence

When your actions, beliefs and values, and identity are fully aligned, and you are fully in harmony with yourself.

Conscious Mind

The part of your mind that you are aware of. See also *Unconscious Mind*.

Content

In any representation (memories, thoughts, stories), content is what the representation is about – as opposed to the structure of how the content is being represented.

Content-Free

Looking at the structure of a statement or story while disregarding the specifics of what the statement or story is about. "There is no content in content worth knowing" - Tad James.

Cross-Matching (also 'crossover matching' or 'crossover mirroring')

Matching some aspect of a person's body language, breathing rhythms etc. with a different part of the body. Usually done because it is less obvious than straight *mirroring*, and is also useful where mirroring would be inappropriate or have damaging side-effects (e.g. tapping a pencil to match an asthmatic breathing pattern instead of mirroring it with your own breathing).

Deletion

The process, often unconscious, of ignoring some of the information available, e.g. not noticing some aspects of sensory input or leaving out some information that we tacitly assume the other person knows when we formulate a spoken sentence.

Digital

1. Describes a representation that is 'coded' and can only be understood if you know the code. E.g. describing something in words is a digital representation; you will only know what is described if you know the language the description is written in. The opposite of *analogue*.

2. Of *submodalities*, describes a submodality that is either one thing or another with no intermediate states – like a switch being on or off, or a computer bit being either one or zero. E.g. one can be either

associated into a memory or *dissociated* from it. There are no intermediate states (although one can alternate between an associated and dissociated representation rapidly). Again, the opposite of *analogue*.

Dissociated

To view a memory or imagined event from the outside, as if you were a detached observer and the event were happening to someone else. This tends to distance you from your feelings about the event more than if you were *associated* into it.

Distortion

The process, often unconscious, of changing information so that it corresponds less closely to external reality – e.g. making links between things that are unrelated, or *mind reading* another person's intentions.

Downtime

Having your attention turned inwards, on your thoughts and/or emotions.

Ecology

In NLP, this means considering the effects of a change on all parts of the wider system.

Elicitation

Discovering some aspects of a person's internal processing, for example their *strategies* or *values*, without altering them either deliberately or accidentally.

Eye Accessing Cues

Movements of a person's eyes in particular directions that indicate *visual*, *auditory* or *kinaesthetic* processing.

First Position

The *perceptual position* corresponding to viewing a situation from your own viewpoint, *associated* into your own thoughts and feelings.

Frame

The boundaries that we draw around our perception of a person, thing, event or concept, which also defines the context in which we view it.

Future Pacing

After making some change, mentally rehearsing what will be different in the relevant situations in the future now that the change has taken place. This is an essential final part of change work, both to check that the intervention has worked, and to set up a link between the 'trigger' of the future event and the new more resourceful response.

Generalisation

The process, often unconscious, of making up rules and expectations based on limited observations.

Gustatory

The sensory modality involving the sense of taste.

'In Time'

When we perceive our *time line* as passing through us, so that 'now' is where we are. Usually, but not in every case, the past is behind us and the future is ahead.

Internal Representation

A person's representation in their mind of the world around them, made up of sensory images and/or internal dialogue and including memories and imagined events as well as processing of sensory input. It bears a similar relation to reality as a map does to the territory that it depicts.

Kinaesthetic

The sensory modality that includes the senses of touch, emotions, balance and proprioception (knowing where each part of your body is in relation to the rest of you).

Leading

You are leading someone else if you do something and they unconsciously mimic it or follow your lead. See also *pacing*.

Lost Performative

A value judgement, stated as if it is an objective fact. Value judgements are made by people, with particular values sets and agendas, but the original 'performer' of the judgement is not referenced – they have been 'lost' from the sentence.

'Logical Levels'

Model developed by Robert Dilts that analyses change in terms of six levels: Environment, Behaviour, Capabilities, Values and Beliefs, Identity, and Spiritual (or Purpose). Usually represented as a hierarchy with Environment at the bottom and Spiritual at the top. Often criticised on the grounds that it's 'content based' and that the levels don't actually form a logical hierarchy, nevertheless it's a useful model.

Matching

When people are in rapport, they tend to unconsciously copy each other's body language, speech rhythms etc. *Matching* is doing this with intent to facilitate rapport – it needs to be done discreetly or it won't be successful. See *Cross-matching, Mirroring*.

Meta Model

The first model of excellence developed by Richard Bandler and John Grinder, derived from their modelling of therapists Virginia Satir and Fritz Perls, codified a set of language patterns that help us recognise various distortions, deletions and generalisations in statements, together with questions designed to recover missing information or invite therapy clients to compare their distortions and generalisations with sensory experience. They called it the Meta Model of language because they believed it would be useful to therapists of any tradition ('meta' is used in this case to mean 'beyond' or 'above').

Meta Model Challenge

A question designed to 'challenge' a *Meta Model violation*, aimed at retrieving deleted information or inviting the 'violator' to check their statement against sensory experience. Perhaps 'violations' and 'challenges' are too adversarial a way of thinking of the Meta Model to be useful in most contexts.

Meta Model Violation

A phrase or sentence that 'violates' the *Meta Model* by containing *deletions*, *distortions* or *generalisations*. You may choose to question it with a *Meta Model challenge*.

Meta programs (also written as meta-programs, metaprograms or metaprogrammes)

The content-free filters that we apply to information, determining which aspects we pay attention to. E.g. a person may habitually focus on the big picture or on details, or their motivation may be primarily towards or away-from. Meta programs may be different in different contexts (e.g. people will tend to be more aware of details for subject areas they are interested in). People can be anywhere on a spectrum of choices for a given meta program, rather than (for example) being *either* 100% reactive or 100% proactive.

Metaphor

Metaphors are analogies that our brain makes up to more easily make sense of information (e.g. 'life is a journey', 'time is money') or by extension, stories that feature elements and events that are analogies to our experience.

Milton Model

A set of trance-inducing 'artfully vague' language patterns modelled by Richard Bandler and John Grinder from the work of the great hypnotherapist Milton Erickson.

Mind Read

A *Meta Model* pattern where the person speaks or acts as if they know for sure what another person is thinking or feeling, e.g. "I know you think I'm wonderful."

Mirroring

A subset of matching where one person matches the posture of another symmetrically, as if they were a mirror image.

Modal Operators

One of the categories of language pattern in the *Meta Model* (and *Milton Model*) indicating unspoken rules about what must or should be done ('Modal

Operators of Necessity') such as should, ought, must, have to; or rules about what can - or can't - be done ('Modal Operators of Possibility' – or 'Impossibility').

Model

In NLP, this can refer to a description of a process or method for achieving a skill that is the output of the *modelling* process; or, slightly confusingly, to the exemplar or 'model of excellence' who is the subject of the modelling process. In the latter sense it's pretty close to the everyday English usage of 'role model'.

Modelling

The heart of NLP – the process of replicating the skill of an exemplar, filtering out the elements that are idiosyncratic to that person, and so reducing the replica to a 'model' that can be taught to others. Most (some would say all) of the techniques in NLP come originally from modelling people who are able to do particular things well.

Nominalisation

A *Meta Model* pattern in which a process is referred to as if it is a thing. So the nominalisation of the process of two people relating to each other would be 'a relationship'. Nominalisations are abstract concepts, often classified as '*deletions*' in the Meta Model because the information regarding the process of relating was lost when it was 'frozen' into 'a relationship'.

Olfactory

The sensory modality involving the sense of smell.

Outcome

Generally used in NLP to be synonymous with 'desired outcome' – i.e. a goal or the result you want to get.

Pacing

Matching another person's body language (or values, preferred sensory modality, social etiquette etc.) as a means to achieving rapport and often as a preliminary to *leading* once rapport has been achieved.

Perceptual Positions

Describes viewing a relationship or disagreement from multiple viewpoints: *first position* is from your own point of view, *second position* is the other person's viewpoint, *third position* is the viewpoint of a detached observer.

Presuppositions

1. Beliefs or assumptions, often unconsciously held, that are embedded in a statement or question without being explicitly stated. In order to make sense of the statement or question, you have to accept the presupposition. The acceptance often also happens outside of conscious awareness.

2. 'Presuppositions of NLP': the primary ideas and assumptions underpinning NLP. The exact wording of these ideas differs slightly from NLP trainer to NLP trainer. You don't have to believe these presuppositions are true, but you pretty much have to act 'as if' they are true in order to get results with NLP.

Primary (or 'Preferred') Representational System

The representational system that a person is mainly using at any given time. This can change depending on context, so avoid classifying people in rigid categories as 'a Visual' or 'a Kinaesthetic'.

Rapport

The process of being in harmony and trust with someone, so that the 'signal to noise' ratio of communication is at its best and messages are received more or less as sent. Some schools of NLP define rapport more in terms of 'getting the attention of the person's unconscious mind', so that it does not necessarily involve mutual liking. For example, if you go to hear someone you admire speak, they will have a degree of 'rapport by reputation' and will not have to work so hard to achieve rapport with the audience as someone previously unknown to them.

Reframing

Representing a statement, thing or event in a different way, which changes our response to it.

Representational System (often called 'rep system' for short)

One of the systems in which we represent and process our experience. These can be sensory modalities (visual, auditory, kinaesthetic, olfactory, and gustatory) or 'digital' representations (usually words).

Resource

A quality or ability that is useful in some context.

Resourceful State

A state in which we have access to the *resources* we need in a given situation. In an unresourceful state such as anxiety or guilt we may be temporarily unable to access the resources we have (e.g. the higher thinking processes of a normally intelligent person may shut down when they are in the throes of road rage).

Second Position

The *perceptual position* corresponding to viewing a relationship or disagreement from the point of view of the other person, helping you to guess at how they might see you and what they might be thinking and feeling.

Sensory Acuity

Noticing what is going on around you via your senses. It is the product of how sharp your senses are, and the quality of attention that you bring to noticing.

Sensory Modalities

The five 'channels' through which we take in and process sensory information, including *visual*, *auditory*, *kinaesthetic* (touch, emotion, balance, and proprioception), *olfactory* (smell) and *gustatory* (taste). Along with the non-sensory 'digital' modality, these are also *representational systems*.

Simple Deletion

A *Meta Model* pattern where part of the information needed to understand a statement is left out. E.g. "I'm so happy" might leave you wondering "About what?"

Stacking Anchors

The process of linking multiple compatible *resource states* to a single stimulus.

State

The ongoing mental and physiological processes within a person at any given time; the totality of their thoughts, feelings and physiology. State can influence a person's memory, learning, and even beliefs.

State-Dependent Memory

This describes the finding that memory retrieval works best when the person is in the same state of consciousness (which can be influenced by factors such as emotion and drugs) as when the memory was originally formed.

Strategy

A sequence of *internal representations* and external sensing and action that consistently leads to a particular outcome. Analogous to computer programs for the brain, strategies (or well-formed ones at least) have a *TOTE Model* structure.

Submodalities (also 'sub-modalities')

The qualities of each *sensory modality* that act like codes to the brain, telling it how much significance to attach to a representation. E.g. with the *visual* submodality of movement, we will generally pay more attention to something that is moving than something that is still.

Third Position

The *perceptual position* corresponding to the viewpoint of a detached observer, helping you to be aware of you and the other person, and the relationship between you, as a whole system.

'Through Time'

When we perceive our *time line* as crossing in front of us so that we are looking 'through' it (usually but not always from left (past) to right (future), and 'now' is some little way ahead of us.

Time Line

The way in which our unconscious minds perceive time and order our memories, by means of a spatial metaphor. In Western societies at least, time is usually spoken of as linear, like a road that we travel along (if we are thought of as moving while time remains still – so 'moving on' or 'leaving the event behind us' or 'looking forward to something happening') or like a river or road that we are standing beside, and events move along from the 'far future' towards us and then flow into the 'distant past' behind us.

TOTE Model

Acronym for "Test, Operate, Test, Exit". The TOTE Model describes the structure of our mental strategies and is derived from Pribram, Miller and Galanter's book *Plans and The Structure of Behaviour* (1960).

Unconscious Mind

The part of your mental processes (actually most of them) that take place outside of conscious awareness. The unconscious mind can be communicated with, influenced, and listened to, most obviously in hypnosis.

Universal Quantifier

A *Meta Model* pattern describing universal generalisations like 'never', 'always', 'everyone', 'everywhere'. Usually extrapolated from a limited number of examples, so a counter-example can usually be found.

Unspecified Referential Index (also Unspecified Noun)

A Meta Model pattern where it is not clear what person, thing or place is being referred to in a statement. E.g. "They're loving this." Maybe who 'they' refers to is clear from the context, maybe it isn't.

Unspecified Verb

A Meta Model pattern in which an action is stated but not specified. This is only a problem if the listener is not clear on what needs to be done. All verbs are unspecified to some extent. E.g. "I want you to fix the problem of climate change" might reasonably invite the question "How specifically do you want me to fix it?"

Uptime

Having your attention entirely focused outside yourself on what is happening around you.

Values

The abstract concepts (with an emotional charge attached) that motivate us, and that act as the criteria by which we decide if something is right or wrong.

Visual

The sensory modality associated with sight and visual processing.

Well-Formed Outcome

A goal or desired result that is specific, measurable, timed, and which the people who have to achieve it are both able and motivated to achieve.

ABOUT THE AUTHOR

Andy Smith is an NLP trainer, Appreciative Inquiry facilitator, and Emotional Intelligence coach who has trained and coached director-level clients in the UK, the Middle East, and South East Asia. He specialises in helping leaders and teams get beyond the blocks that stop them achieving their potential. Andy is the author of *Achieve Your Goals: Strategies to Transform Your Life* (Dorling Kindersley 2006) and the *Practical NLP, Practical Coaching Guides* and *Quick Personal Development* e-book series. To see all of Andy's books and e-books, visit the Practical NLP website at nlppod.com.

Andy is a serial NLP practice group founder. He started the Richmond NLP Group (along with Nick Driscoll) in 1996 and it's still going strong, having been through a couple of changes of management. He also started the Manchester NLP Group and the Manchester Business NLP and Emotional Intelligence Group, all of which have given countless people their first step on their NLP journey.

ABOUT THE AUTHOR

As well as the Practical NLP e-book series, Andy has developed an acclaimed activity pack for NLP trainers, *The NLP Trainer's Exercise Pack*, as well as customisable and rebrandable NLP course manuals that will save newly-qualified trainers weeks of effort. You can find these resources at: webstore.coachingleaders.co.uk.

Website, blog and podcast: nlppod.com

My 'other' site, for information and tips about Appreciative Inquiry, coaching, emotional intelligence and leadership: coachingleaders.co.uk

Online store: webstore.coachingleaders.co.uk

Twitter: @PracticalNLP

Contact: andy@coachingleaders.co.uk

BOOKS BY ANDY SMITH

Want to be informed of future releases? Register your interest at:

nlppod.com/subscribe

And find the most up-to-date list of my books at: nlppod.com/books

Practical NLP Series

Practical NLP: How to Use NLP Principles to Improve Your Life and Work, Even if You're Not NLP Trained

Practical NLP 2: Language - How to Use Presuppositions, Chunking, the Meta Model and the Milton Model in Practice

Practical NLP 3: Sensory Acuity and Rapport

Practical NLP 4: Submodalities and Anchoring

Practical NLP 5: Strategies

Practical NLP 6: Parts, Frames, and Reframing

Practical NLP 7: Business and Leadership

BOOKS BY ANDY SMITH

Practical NLP 8: Values, Goals, and Timelines

Practical Coaching Guides

How to Work With the SCORE Model

15 Exercises for Training Listening Skills and Rapport

Practical EQ Series

How to Lead with Emotional Intelligence

The Smart Way to Hire Emotionally Intelligent People Without Using Expensive Assessments, and Minimise Unconscious Bias in Your Recruitment Processes

55 Ways to Increase Your Emotional Intelligence

www.ingramcontent.com/pod-product-compliance
Lightning Source LLC
Chambersburg PA
CBHW020433220526
45464CB00002B/684